Daily
Skill-Builders

Grammar & Usage

Grades 5-6

DISCARDED

Writer
Sarah Guare

Editorial Director
Susan A. Blair

Project Manager
Erica L. Varney

Cover Designer
Roman Laszok

Interior Designer
Mark Sayer

Production Editor
Maggie Jones

WALCH PUBLISHING

The classroom teacher may reproduce copies of materials in this book for classroom use only.

The reproduction of any part for an entire school or school system is strictly prohibited.

No part of this publication may be transmitted, stored, or recorded in any form without written

permission from the publisher.

1   2   3   4   5   6   7   8   9   10

ISBN 0-8251-4784-0

Copyright © 2004

Walch Publishing

P. O. Box 658 • Portland, Maine 04104-0658

walch.com

Printed in the United States of America

Table of Contents

Daily Skill-Builders

Grammar & Usage

Grades 5–6

To the Teacher

Introduction to *Daily Skill-Builders*

The *Daily Skill-Builders* series began as an expansion of our popular *Daily Warm-Ups* series for grades 5–adult. Word spread, and eventually elementary teachers were asking for something similar. Just as *Daily Warm-Ups* do, *Daily Skill-Builders* turn extra classroom minutes into valuable learning time. Not only do these activities reinforce necessary skills for elementary students, they also make skill-drilling an engaging and informative process. Each book in this series contains 180 reproducible activities—one for each day of the school year!

How to Use *Daily Skill-Builders*

Daily Skill-Builders are easy to use—simply photocopy the day's activity and distribute it. Each page is designed to take approximately ten to fifteen minutes. Many teachers choose to use them in the morning when students are arriving at school or in the afternoon before students leave for the day. They are also a great way to switch gears from one subject to another. No matter how you choose to use them, extra classroom minutes will never go unused again.

Building Skills for All Students

The *Daily Skill-Builders* activities give you great flexibility. The activities can be used effectively in a variety of ways to help all your students develop important skills, regardless of their level.

Depending on the needs of your students and your curriculum goals, you may want the entire class to do the same skill-builder, or you may select specific activities for different students. There are several activities for each

topic covered in *Daily Skill-Builders*, so you can decide which and how many activities to use to help students to master a particular skill.

If a student does not complete an activity in the allotted time, he or she may complete it as homework, or you may allow more time the next day to finish. If a student completes a skill-builder early, you may want to assign another. *Daily Skill-Builders* give you options that work for you.

Students in one grade level vary in their abilities, so each *Daily Skill-Builders* covers two grades. In a fourth-grade class, for example, some students may need the books for grades 3–4. Other students may need the greater challenge presented in the 4–5 books. Since all the books look virtually the same and many of the activities are similar, the students need not know that they are working at different levels.

No matter how you choose to use them, *Daily Skill-Builders* will enhance your teaching. They are easy for you to use, and your students will approach them positively as they practice needed skills.

Places to Go, People to See!

A **common noun** names a nonspecific person, place, thing, or idea. It is not capitalized.

Examples: dentist **(person)**, school **(place)**, crayon **(thing)**, emotion **(idea)**

Write common nouns on the lines below to complete the sentences. The first one has been done for you.

1. Our _____car_____ (thing) is very fast on the highway.

2. We got lost going to the _____ (place), so we decided not to go.

3. The _____ (person) gave a wonderful concert.

4. My _____ (idea) are easily hurt when my friends are mean to me.

5. My _____ (person) taught me how to fish and ride a bike.

6. The _____ (thing) wasn't large enough to cover my head.

7. We should put the papers inside the _____ (thing).

8. We saw a giraffe at the _____ (place).

9. The _____ (person) graded my homework.

10. Everyone wants the _____ (idea) to do what they want.

Catch a Common Noun

A **common noun** refers to a nonspecific person, place, thing, or idea. It is not capitalized.

Examples: astronaut **(person)**, town **(place)**, desk **(thing)**, happiness **(idea)**

Read the common nouns below. For each, think of two more common nouns that are related to it. Write the words on the lines below. The first one has been done for you.

1. clown

   circus

   elephant

2. doctor

3. coat

4. doll

5. joy

6. camp

7. bakery

8. soup

9. country

10. classroom

11. ocean

12. chef

Daily Skill-Builders Grammar & Usage 5–6
walch.com © 2004 Walch Publishing

Go Fly a Kite!

A **proper noun** names a specific person, place, thing, or idea. It is always capitalized.

Examples: Mrs. Randolph **(person),** Toronto **(place),**
Martha's Blonde Brownies **(thing),** United Nations **(idea)**

For each of the underlined common nouns in the story below, think of a proper noun or nouns that could replace it. Write the proper nouns above the common nouns. Complete the last paragraph of the story and underline the proper nouns you use.

My Flowered Kite

Yesterday was a gorgeous summer day. The birds were chirping, the flowers were blooming, and <u>children</u> were playing outside. It was so beautiful that <u>a girl</u> decided it would be a good day to go to <u>the park</u> and fly a kite. <u>The girl</u> went with <u>her brother</u> and <u>a friend</u>.

The <u>girl's</u> father had just bought a kite from <u>the store</u> for her birthday. It was a large green kite with a long, white tail and a picture of a flower printed on the front. It was so beautiful that she named it <u>kite</u>. She didn't want <u>her brother</u> and <u>her friend</u> to play with <u>kite</u>, but she knew that she had to share it.

<u>The kite</u> flew high. It flew over <u>the street.</u> It flew over <u>the store</u>. It flew beside <u>the lighthouse</u>. It flew above the crowds of people at <u>the beach</u>. It flew above <u>the ocean.</u> <u>Kite</u> kept flying higher and higher and farther away. It flew

Acting Proper

A **proper noun** names a specific person, place, thing, or idea. It is always capitalized.

For each common noun below, think of two other proper nouns that are related to it. Write the words on the lines below. The first one has been done for you.

1. café

   _____Red Door Café_____

   Grandma's Homebaked Cookies

2. women

   _____

   _____

3. national park

   _____

   _____

4. newspaper

   _____

   _____

5. sports figure

   _____

   _____

6. shops

   _____

   _____

7. state

   _____

   _____

8. men

   _____

   _____

9. school

   _____

   _____

10. city

   _____

   _____

Daily Skill·Builders Grammar & Usage 5–6
walch.com © 2004 Walch Publishing

Ups and Downs of Nouns

A **common noun** refers to a nonspecific person, place, thing, or idea. A **proper noun** refers to a specific person, place, thing, or idea. Proper nouns are capitalized.

Examples: waiter, store, scooter, love **(common nouns)**
Dr. Marshall, Asia, Liberty Bell, Baptist **(proper nouns)**

Underline the common nouns once. Underline the proper nouns twice and capitalize them.

1. My nurse at johnson county hospital, mrs. harnett, was very nice.

2. The last movie I saw, <u>spot's great adventure</u>, was very funny.

3. I bought a sweater and a hat at sarah's boutique.

4. We took the train into the city of chicago.

5. She bought apples, oranges, and bananas at harry's market.

6. I think that jealousy can be a very intense emotion.

7. mrs. danby told george to clean the table in the corner.

8. the waves at ferry beach were huge!

9. I think that mount everest is the tallest mountain in the world.

10. His jacket kept him dry in seattle.

11. We took a break from practicing our music.

12. The band's latest album, <u>bright room</u>, is terrific!

Classifying Nouns

Nouns are words that name a person, a place, a thing, or an idea. The following nouns name a person or a place. Underline the nouns in each sentence.

1. The pilot talked loudly.

2. Aunt Harriet snores, especially when she's tired.

3. Hinkley Park is so big that I became lost there once.

4. George said he liked to go swimming.

5. The Empire State Building is very, very tall.

A **concrete noun** names something that can be either seen or touched.

    Examples: mountain, desk, apple, cloud

An **abstract noun** names something that can't be seen or touched.

    Examples: love, anger, sadness, peace

Underline the nouns in the following sentences. On the line, tell if the underlined noun is concrete (**C**) or abstract (**A**).

6. The ball was blue, yellow, and green. _____

7. The flag was upside down. _____

8. That gave me joy. _____

9. The sun is very bright. _____

10. I don't like to feel hatred. _____

11. His spirit is still with us. _____

12. The sled was too small to fit all of them. _____

13. Her surprise was obvious. _____

14. The hammer worked very well. _____

15. I feel a lot of love for my older brother. _____

A Flock of Nouns

A **collective noun** names a collection of persons, animals, or things.

Examples: band, flock, colony

Use a collective noun to complete each sentence below.

1. A group of students is a _____.

2. A group of sports players is a _____.

3. A group of puppies is a _____.

4. A group of cows is a _____.

5. A group of cookies is a _____.

6. A group of relatives is a _____.

7. A group of wolves is a _____.

Complete each sentence below. Use a dictionary if needed.

8. A chorus is a group of _____.

9. A constellation is a group of _____.

10. A gaggle is a group of _____.

11. A troop is a group of _____.

12. A school is a group of _____.

13. A deck is a group of _____.

14. An army is a group of _____.

A Bunch of Balloons

A **collective noun** names a collection of persons, animals, or things.

Draw a circle around each of the collective nouns in the sentences below.

1. The bouquet of roses looks beautiful on the dining room table.

2. We could hear the pack of wolves howling in the woods.

3. There was a gaggle of geese near the pond this morning.

4. I love carrots, so I dug a bunch from our garden.

5. The fleet of ships is headed across the Atlantic Ocean on a mission.

6. This restaurant has the nicest staff of waiters and waitresses.

7. One puppy is great, but a whole litter is a handful!

8. My parents made a large batch of brownies for the bake sale.

9. I gave a Valentine's Day card to everyone in my class.

10. The colony of ants took away my peanut butter sandwich!

11. The band had a drummer, a guitarist, and a saxophone player.

12. We planted flowers near the grove of trees in the backyard.

13. The audience applauded for the talented musician.

14. We learned to create an array of numbers on the computer.

15. Jim and I ate a large cluster of grapes.

Daily Skill-Builders Grammar & Usage 5–6
walch.com © 2004 Walch Publishing

Beach Collections

A **collective noun** names a collection of persons, places, or things.

Replace each underlined noun below with the appropriate collective noun from the box. Write the word on the line.

colony	herd	class	flock	fleet
family	forest	band	team	bouquet

1. The <u>musicians</u> played music on the boardwalk. _____

2. There was a <u>seagulls</u> of birds near the water. _____

3. The <u>students</u> took a field trip to the beach. _____

4. The <u>ants</u> came and took away the rest of my apple. _____

5. I picked a <u>wild roses</u> to give to my mother. _____

6. My <u>relatives</u> likes to vacation on the beach. _____

7. We saw the <u>ships</u> pull into the harbor. _____

8. Sometimes, the <u>soccer players</u> practices on the beach. _____

9. There is a <u>trees</u> near the ocean. _____

10. We never see a <u>cows</u> on the beach. _____

Plural Noun Stars

To make some nouns plural, add an **s.**

Examples: tables, straws, radios

Write the plural form of each noun on the line.

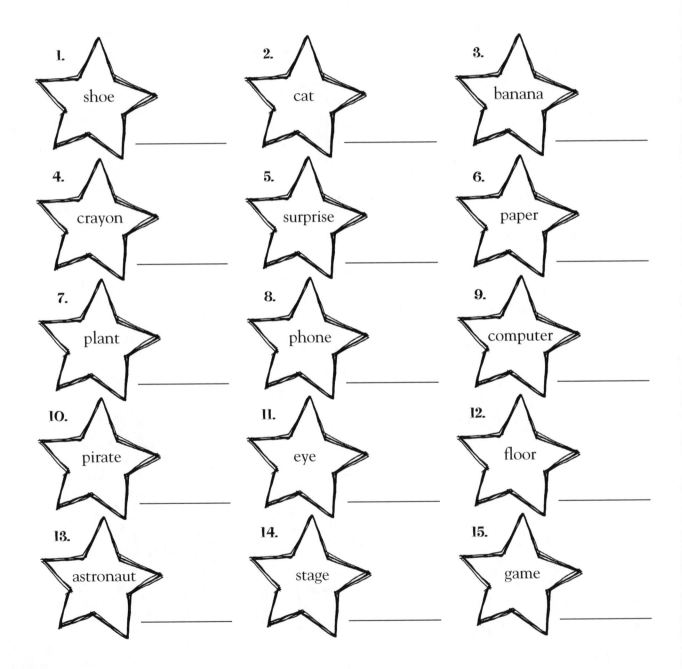

1. shoe

2. cat

3. banana

4. crayon

5. surprise

6. paper

7. plant

8. phone

9. computer

10. pirate

11. eye

12. floor

13. astronaut

14. stage

15. game

Plural Pops

Singular nouns that end in **ch, sh, x, s,** or **z** can be made plural by adding **es** to the end of the word.

Circle the number of the lollipops below that take this rule. Write the plural form of the noun on the lines.

1. patch _____

2. tax _____

3. dress _____

4. rash _____

5. elastic _____

6. watch _____

7. duck _____

8. glass _____

9. milk _____

10. waltz _____

More Than One

Most **nouns** are made plural by adding **s** or **es.**

Write the plural form of each word on the line. The first one has been done for you.

1. store

   stores

2. bench

   _____

3. camera

   _____

4. mall

   _____

5. dress

   _____

6. witch

   _____

7. patch

   _____

8. cup

   _____

9. peach

   _____

10. class

    _____

11. desk

    _____

12. garden

    _____

13. car

    _____

14. fox

    _____

15. basket

    _____

Change Y to I

To make a noun that ends in **y** plural, cross out the **y** and add **ies**.

Example: pupp/ +**ies** → puppies

For each of the words below, write the plural form on the line. The first one has been done for you.

1. party _____parties_____

2. family _____

3. mystery _____

4. poppy _____

5. pony _____

6. policy _____

7. assembly _____

8. disability _____

9. community _____

10. dairy _____

11. comedy _____

12. cherry _____

A Flock of V's and a Bunch of O's

The plural of most nouns ending in **f** or **fe** is formed by adding **s.** For some nouns that end in **f** or **fe,** the **f** is changed to a **v** and an **s** or **es** is added.

Examples: gulf, gulfs; leaf, leaves

Write the plural form of the nouns on the lines. Use a dictionary, if needed.

1. scarf _____

2. roof _____

3. life _____

4. wife _____

5. wharf _____

6. cliff _____

For nouns that end in **o,** add an **s.** For nouns that have a consonant before the **o,** add **es.**

Examples: studio, studios; tomato, tomatoes

Write the plural form of the nouns on the lines.

7. potato _____

8. radio _____

9. domino _____

10. patio _____

11. tomato _____

12. studio _____

Daily Skill-Builders Grammar & Usage 5–6
walch.com © 2004 Walch Publishing

Name _____

Spot the Difference

Not all nouns are made plural by adding an **s** or **es.** Nouns that do not form plurals with **s** or **es** are called **irregular nouns.** These are best learned through practice.

Write the plural form of each noun on each line. Circle the number of the spots that contain irregular nouns. Use a dictionary, if needed.

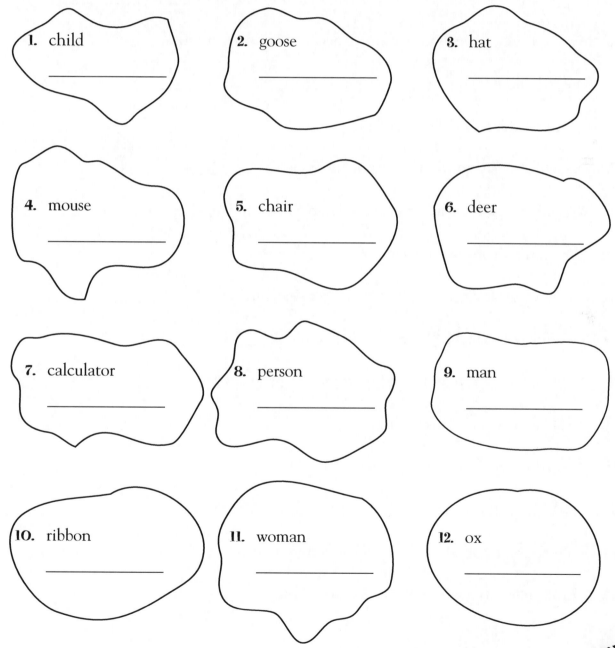

1. child _____

2. goose _____

3. hat _____

4. mouse _____

5. chair _____

6. deer _____

7. calculator _____

8. person _____

9. man _____

10. ribbon _____

11. woman _____

12. ox _____

Yours or Mine?

Possessive nouns show ownership. You can make most nouns possessive by adding an **apostrophe** and an **s** to the noun.

Find the noun in each sentence below that should be made possessive. Write the possessive form of the noun on the line next to each sentence.

1. The puppy bone is near the tree in the corner of the yard. _____

2. My Uncle Charlie recipe won first place at a baking contest. _____

3. The girl dress was sopping wet when she came home. _____

4. I can hear the lady radio blasting next door. _____

5. One quiet, misty morning, we found a fox den. _____

6. Women everywhere can appreciate Susan B. Anthony courage. _____

7. Our country highways are very safe. _____

8. A teacher dream is to see all of his or her students succeed. _____

9. My grandfather life in Poland was very difficult. _____

10. A carpenter job is to build and fix things for people. _____

11. A friend job is to be a good listener. _____

12. We had the cook special for lunch at the diner. _____

13. The cute, little duckling feet were almost too small to notice. _____

14. The magazine published the scientist latest discovery. _____

15. We all suffer from writer block at some point. _____

Whose Is It?

Possessive nouns show ownership. To make most plural nouns possessive, just add an **apostrophe.** For irregular plural nouns, add an **apostrophe** and an **s.**

   Examples: two **girls'** books; the **team's** coach

Make each underlined noun possessive. Write the possessive form on the line.

1. The <u>children</u> theater is giving a performance tonight. _____

2. The <u>actors</u> fans are waiting outside the dressing rooms. _____

3. The <u>people</u> choice for president was Ronald Morgan. _____

4. My <u>parents</u> choice didn't win the election. _____

5. The <u>geese</u> homes are by the pond. _____

6. The <u>ducks</u> eggs are speckled brown. _____

7. The <u>fawns</u> legs are very thin. _____

8. The <u>deer</u> tracks are everywhere. _____

9. The <u>birds</u> nests are in those two trees. _____

10. The <u>mice</u> nests are in the corner of the garage. _____

11. The <u>women</u> team won the gold cup. _____

12. The <u>players</u> coach was very excited. _____

Are They Together?

A **possessive noun** shows ownership. When two nouns are together in a sentence, make the second noun possessive to show shared ownership. Make both nouns possessive to show separate ownerships. Be sure to add an apostrophe and an **s.**

> **Examples:** Julia and Tim's party is next Wednesday. **(shared ownership)**
> (Both Julia and Tim are throwing the party.)
> Julia's and Tim's parties are next week. **(separate ownership)**
> (Julia and Tim are having separate parties.)

Make the nouns below possessive according to what each sentence says. The first one has been done for you.

1. Mike and Christy's parents are retired from the law profession. (shared)

2. Robin   and Casey   books are on the bookshelf. (shared)

3. Miguel   and Juan   sisters are going to the beach with them. (separate)

4. Mrs. Humphrey   and Mr. Bartlett   children are going on the field trip. (separate)

5. We should bring my mom   and dad   flashlight with us. (shared)

6. Lewis   and Clark   trip was very interesting. (shared)

7. Lewis   and Clark   feelings about the trip were very similar. (separate)

8. The doctor   and nurse   decision was the right one. (shared)

9. The coach   and the player   expectations were different. (separate)

10. Bernie   and Lucas   project will be on display in the hallway. (shared)

11. Tracy   and Jonathan   snow fort is in the front yard. (shared)

12. We should take Rob   and Molly   homework for them. (separate)

Pair Them Up!

Certain **nouns** are often **abbreviated**. Draw lines from the nouns below to their abbreviations. Think of two other nouns that are commonly abbreviated. Write the nouns and their abbreviations on the lines.

1.	corporation	a.	gal.
2.	avenue	b.	univ.
3.	century	c.	assn.
4.	incorporated	d.	capt.
5.	gallon	e.	ave.
6.	population	f.	corp.
7.	association	g.	dept.
8.	captain	h.	subj.
9.	university	i.	st.
10.	division	j.	inc.
11.	second(s)	k.	vol.
12.	department	l.	ex.
13.	governor	m.	cent.
14.	street	n.	div.
15.	volume	o.	sec.
16.	subject	p.	gov.
17.	attorney	q.	pop.
18.	example	r.	atty.
19.	_____		_____
20.	_____		_____

Shorten Them!

Some **nouns** can be **abbreviated**. States, streets, titles, months, and days of the week are often abbreviated. Some abbreviations end with a period and some do not.

Examples: NC = North Carolina   **Mr.** = Mister   **St.** = Street
(or **N.C.**)   **Mon.** = Monday   **Mar.** = March

Look at each term. Write its abbreviation on the line. Use a dictionary, if needed.

Term	Abbreviation
1. Vermont	_____
2. Doctor	_____
3. Avenue	_____
4. Wednesday	_____
5. Nebraska	_____
6. October	_____
7. Hawaii	_____
8. Boulevard	_____
9. Senior	_____
10. Dentist	_____
11. Reverend	_____
12. Senator	_____
13. Professor	_____
14. New York	_____
15. Lieutenant	_____

Daily Skill-Builders Grammar & Usage 5–6
walch.com © 2004 Walch Publishing

Measure Up!

Mathematical and **measurement terms** are often **abbreviated**. Terms from the customary measurement system use a period, but terms from the metric (international) measurement system do not.

> **Examples: ft.** = feet, **oz.** = ounce **(customary system)**
> **cm** = centimeter, **kg** = kilogram **(metric system)**

Look at each term. Write its abbreviation on the line. Use a dictionary, if needed.

Term	Abbreviation
1. pound	_____
2. cup	_____
3. milligram	_____
4. gross	_____
5. yard	_____
6. inch	_____
7. pint	_____
8. acre	_____
9. quart	_____
10. revolutions per minute	_____
11. gallon	_____
12. miles per hour	_____
13. fluid ounce	_____
14. millimeter	_____
15. meter	_____

Athletic Actions

An **action verb** tells what the subject is doing.

Examples: Judy and Cameron **rolled** the marbles across the pavement.
Jordan **sings** in the shower.

Complete each sentence with the correct word from the word box below.

stands	flip	threw	fold	tosses	run
catches	swings	hit	bounced	jumped	kicked

1. Mia _____ the ball into the net.

2. The goalie _____ the ball onto the field.

3. The ball _____ off Courtney's head.

4. Jason _____ the ball very high when he serves.

5. Margie _____ very close to the net when she volleys.

6. Chelsea always _____ at the ball.

7. The third baseman always _____ the ball.

8. The batter _____ a homerun.

9. Nomar can _____ the bases very quickly.

10. Did you see Greg _____ over backward?

11. The gymnast _____ high into the air.

12. The girl who won could _____ herself into the shape of a pretzel.

Daily Skill-Builders Grammar & Usage 5–6
walch.com © 2004 Walch Publishing

Follow the Action!

An **action verb** tells what the subject is doing.

    Examples: The girl **jumps** over the rope.

               The girl **swings** the rope over her head.

Underline the action verbs in the sentences below.

1. The builder hammered a nail into the wall.

2. The man shuffled the deck of cards like an experienced player.

3. The boys hopped over every crack in the sidewalk.

4. We fixed the lights in the theater.

5. My sister sings in the choir on Saturday.

6. We brought the rest of the chocolate pies.

7. The weeds outside grow very quickly.

8. The wagon fell over on its side.

9. We sprayed water on our coach after the game.

10. The candle burned a hole through the paper.

11. My phone rings constantly at home.

12. The little kitten batted my ball of yarn.

13. I ride my horse Target every weekend.

14. The wind blew the papers across the lawn.

15. We picked strawberries on the farm.

Take Action!

An **action verb** tells what the subject is doing.

Write an action verb on each line below to describe the circus.

1. The tightrope performers _____ across a very high wire.

2. Ten clowns _____ into a very tiny car and drove away.

3. The magician _____ two rabbits out of his hat.

4. We _____ lots of cotton candy and popcorn at the circus.

5. The tigers _____ loudly at the audience.

6. We saw elephants _____ on two legs.

7. I saw a man _____ fire out of his mouth.

Choose the verbs below to describe what a firefighter does. Use one action verb in each sentence.

sprays	drives	climbs	carries	searches	saves

8. _____

_____

9. _____

_____

10. _____

_____

Daily Skill-Builders Grammar & Usage 5–6
walch.com © 2004 Walch Publishing

Connect the Caboose

A **linking verb** connects the subject to a noun or an adjective that follows it.

Examples: We **are** very tired tonight.
The squid **tastes** delicious.

Complete the sentences below with the following linking verbs.

were	am	smell	turn	appears
seems	looks	is	being	feels
grow	sounds	tastes	remain	are

1. The roses in the backyard _____ very good.

2. The animal in the yard _____ to be a raccoon.

3. The foghorn _____ very eerie at night.

4. The pasta _____ like my mom's pasta.

5. I _____ happy to see my grandparents again.

6. Those leaves will _____ orange in the fall.

7. Thank-you for _____ a good neighbor.

8. My bike will _____ locked up until I can find the key.

9. They _____ frightened to see the wolves.

10. The dough _____ very sticky.

11. My cousin may _____ tall like his father.

12. Your puppy _____ the cutest pet I've ever seen.

13. Your new skirt _____ pretty.

14. They _____ the nicest people.

15. Your skin _____ paler in the light.

What's Missing?

A **linking verb** connects the subject with a noun or an adjective that follows it.

Examples: She **is** happy to be finished with her project.
The music **sounds** good.

Draw a caret or insert mark (**^**) where each sentence is missing a linking verb. Write the missing verb above the sentence. Use the linking verbs in the box below.

become	am	were	appeared	looks
turn	seems	feel	tastes	is

1. The homemade ice cream delicious.

2. The bananas will brown if you leave them there.

3. My scooter very old.

4. The runner very tired at the end of the race.

5. The new car shiny in the sunlight.

6. I excited to go to a foreign country.

7. The speaker nervous.

8. The stale cookies hard.

9. The tadpoles will frogs.

10. The players tired after the long game.

I'm Late!

A **helping verb** is used with the main verb to express different times and moods. Some helping verbs include **has, had,** and **have; do** and **did;** and forms of the verb **to be** such as **am, is, was,** and **were.**

Examples: Jason **will** play in the game this afternoon.

I **have** taken three flowers from the bouquet.

Help this boy apologize to his mother for being late for dinner. Use the helping verbs in the box below to complete each sentence.

may	must	am	could	had	will
would	did	were	should	can	shall

1. I'm sorry; I know that I _____ call when I'm going to be late.

2. I _____ to go over to Eric's house to help him with his homework.

3. I _____ not know that it was so late.

4. I _____ have called if I had known it was past six o'clock.

5. We _____ working very hard.

6. I _____ have forgotten to check my watch.

7. Next time, I _____ be sure to look at the clock.

8. You _____ also call Eric's house to remind me.

9. I know that I _____ being irresponsible when I don't call.

10. If you'd like, I _____ come home right after school tomorrow.

11. I _____ make dinner; Eric's mom taught me how to make spaghetti.

12. We _____ see if I am a good cook.

Helping Hands

A **helping verb** helps the main verb of a sentence.

> **Examples:** I **will** try to hit a homerun next time.
> We **may** not win the game.

Underline the helping verbs in the sentences below.

1. The sun may appear this afternoon.
2. The boys will bring the heavy pile of wood over here.
3. The mice have built a nest in our garage.
4. I am going to the store to buy an orange ball.
5. Cathy can lift three chairs with one hand.
6. I could help you bring these to the car.
7. They are bringing five suitcases and two duffle bags.
8. We should eat at Jerry's Restaurant.
9. Yves and Jackie must remember to bring their watches.
10. He has brought us some treats.

Now, use the helping verbs from the sentences above to answer the following questions.

11. Would you like a lifetime supply of noodles?

    _____

12. Can you carry those bags on your own?

    _____

13. Will you know what to do if you get lost?

    _____

14. Are you going to take a long nap?

    _____

15. Do you think it was right for the boys to leave without saying good-bye?

    _____

Daily Skill-Builders Grammar & Usage 5–6
walch.com © 2004 Walch Publishing

To Link or to Help?

A **linking verb** connects a subject with a noun or an adjective that follows it. A **helping verb** helps the main verb.

Circle the linking verbs below. Draw an arrow from the subject to the noun or adjective that the linking verb connects it to.

1. The music in the movie sounded terrific.

2. The oranges in the basket feel soft.

3. I am surprised to see you up so early.

4. The substitute seems very strict.

5. Our moms are very good cooks.

6. The fresh tomatoes taste sweet.

7. The road looks slippery.

8. They are kind to their injured friend.

9. My hair turns blond in the sun.

10. My aunt became a lawyer.

Circle the helping verbs below. Underline the verbs they are helping.

11. I must feed my rabbit this morning.

12. I should buy my mother a birthday gift.

13. I can recite all of the state capitals.

14. You may bring your radio on the bus.

15. I would make dinner if I had the time.

16. I am playing soccer in the fall.

17. My father has given me permission to come.

18. I could give you the keys when I leave.

19. She is helping her dad move.

20. I will write to you next week.

Past, Present, and Future

The **tense** of a **verb** is its time. The **present tense** tells that an action is _happening now_ or is _happening regularly_. The **past tense** tells that an action _happened at a specific time in the past_. The **future tense** tells that an action _will happen in the future_.

Underline the verbs in the following sentences. Write the correct tense on the line.

1. I will read those two books. _____

2. My cat chases its tail every day. _____

3. We went to the circus on Saturday. _____

4. He listens to his favorite song. _____

5. I protected my books from the rain. _____

6. We will meet my friend at the movies. _____

7. Nora looks for her cat under her bed every night. _____

8. I always guess the correct number of jelly beans. _____

9. I ate breakfast early this morning. _____

10. I grabbed the last peanut butter cookie. _____

11. Gophers dig holes in our backyard. _____

12. We crawled under the picket fence. _____

13. My parents will attend the awards ceremony. _____

14. My dog once chewed through a plastic ball. _____

15. I will have a fun party for my birthday. _____

Time Travel

The **tense** of a verb is its time. The **present tense** tells that an action is *happening now* or is *happening regularly*. The **past tense** tells that an action *happened at a specific time in the past*. The **future tense** tells that an action *will happen in the future*.

Write a sentence for each tense of the verbs below. One sentence in each group has been done for you.

1. **Present:** I **mow** the lawn every week for my dad. _____

   Past: _____

   Future: _____

2. **Present:** _____

   Past: _____

   Future: I **will climb** the tallest oak tree tomorrow. _____

3. **Present:** _____

   Past: We **moved** into this house five years ago. _____

   Future: _____

4. **Present:** _____

   Past: _____

   Future: I hope that I **will live** to be a hundred years old. _____

5. **Present:** We **skate** on the pond in the park every winter. _____

   Past: _____

   Future: _____

A Trip to the Desert

Write the correct **tenses** of the **verbs** on the lines below.

A Desert Trip

We sometimes **1.**_____ through the desert when we **2.**_____
‎ ‎ ‎ ‎ ‎ ‎ ‎ ‎ ‎ ‎ to drive ‎ to visit

my cousins. We always **3.**_____ cacti and birds. It's fun to watch the birds
‎ ‎ ‎ ‎ ‎ ‎ ‎ ‎ ‎ ‎ ‎ ‎ ‎ ‎ ‎ ‎ to see

because some of them **4.**_____ very large. The thing that I **5.**_____
‎ ‎ ‎ ‎ ‎ ‎ ‎ ‎ ‎ ‎ ‎ ‎ ‎ ‎ ‎ ‎ ‎ to be ‎ to like

most about the desert, though, is the sand. When the sun **6.**_____ at night,
‎ to set

the sand is a beautiful dark-red color.

I can **7.**_____ the first time I **8.**_____ the rich color of the
‎ ‎ ‎ ‎ ‎ ‎ ‎ to remember ‎ ‎ ‎ ‎ ‎ ‎ ‎ ‎ ‎ ‎ ‎ ‎ to see

sand. I was ten when we **9.**_____ across the desert for the first time. I
‎ ‎ ‎ ‎ ‎ ‎ ‎ ‎ ‎ ‎ ‎ ‎ ‎ ‎ ‎ ‎ to travel

10._____ as though I was in a movie. The cacti **11.**_____ so large and
‎ ‎ ‎ to feel ‎ to be

the sand **12.**_____ so beautiful that I **13.**_____ it couldn't be real. I
‎ ‎ ‎ ‎ ‎ ‎ ‎ ‎ to be ‎ ‎ ‎ ‎ ‎ ‎ ‎ ‎ ‎ ‎ ‎ ‎ to think

14._____ out the car window and **15.**_____ nothing for miles.
‎ ‎ ‎ to stare ‎ ‎ ‎ ‎ ‎ ‎ ‎ ‎ ‎ ‎ ‎ ‎ ‎ ‎ ‎ ‎ ‎ to say

We **16.**_____ to my cousins' house again in a few weeks. My grandfather
‎ ‎ ‎ ‎ ‎ ‎ to go

17._____ with us, along with my brother and my two sisters. It
‎ ‎ to come

18._____ a full car. We **19.**_____ along gifts for my cousin. My
‎ ‎ ‎ to be ‎ ‎ ‎ ‎ ‎ ‎ ‎ ‎ ‎ ‎ ‎ to bring

grandfather **20.**_____ two treasure chests for my cousins next week. My
‎ ‎ ‎ ‎ ‎ ‎ ‎ ‎ to make

parents **21.**_____ some things for them at the fair on Sunday. They miss the
‎ ‎ ‎ ‎ ‎ ‎ to buy

ocean, so we **22.**_____ beach souvenirs. The trip **23.**_____ lots of fun,
‎ ‎ ‎ ‎ to purchase ‎ ‎ ‎ ‎ ‎ ‎ ‎ ‎ ‎ ‎ ‎ ‎ ‎ to be

and I can't wait!

Daily Skill-Builders Grammar & Usage 5–6
walch.com © 2004 Walch Publishing

Who or What?

A **direct object** receives the action of an action verb. It answers the question _what?_ or _whom?_

> **Example:** Richard **dumped** <u>water</u> in the hole.
>   (_Dumped_ is the action verb, and _water_ is the direct object.)

Circle the action verbs below. Underline the direct objects.

1. Rebecca tied a bow in her sister's hair.

2. We sang tunes during the long car ride.

3. Ursula drove a boat for the first time.

4. They give stickers to everyone who comes.

5. My mother likes fresh flowers in a vase.

6. We traced pictures in the sand.

7. Mrs. Barnacle sells sandglass by the seashore.

8. Miguel races cars for a living.

9. I stuck the note to the side of the refrigerator.

10. We planted tomatoes, cucumbers, and radishes in our garden.

11. The doctor checked my throat for spots.

12. My uncles tell funny stories.

13. The crickets made noises all night long.

14. The artist carves statues out of marble.

15. My dog sniffed a skunk, and now my dog stinks.

Direct Me to Your Object

A **direct object** receives the action of an action verb. A direct object answers the question *who?* or *what?*

> **Example:** Malcolm **read** the <u>poem</u> aloud to the class.
> (*Read* is the action verb, and *poem* is the direct object.)

Complete each sentence with a word from the box. If the word is a direct object, circle the word.

pants	cherries	bikes	back	fireflies
ear	tree	bubbles	boat	rocks

1. We rode our _____ to the store.

2. We catch _____ at night.

3. We blew _____ at the beach.

4. The birds sing when they are in the _____.

5. We rowed the _____ safely to the shore.

6. I ate until my _____ were too tight to button!

7. I whispered in his _____, but he couldn't hear me.

8. We like the _____ along the edge of the pond.

9. I floated on my _____ down the river.

10. We ate _____ after dinner.

I Object!

An **indirect object** names the person for whom or to whom something is done.

> **Example:** We gave **Jody** a surprise party.
>
> (*Jody* is the indirect object for whom the party is given.)

Circle the action verbs in the sentences below. Underline the indirect objects.

1. The librarian informed us of the fee for overdue books.

2. The doctor gave Cindy medicine.

3. Leo showed us the waltz.

4. Abbey told the crowd a funny joke.

5. The neighbors left Jane a pie.

6. Cameron brought us the scooter.

7. Sydney told me a secret.

8. My cousin sent me a postcard.

9. The man wrote his friend a long letter.

10. The official promised the runners a good dinner.

11. My dad caught me a big fish.

12. The poet read me his favorite line.

13. My mother made us dinner.

14. Marc played me his favorite song.

15. He promised Janet a ride on the roller coaster.

Name _____

What's Your Profession?

An **indirect object** names the person to whom or for whom something is done.

Example: The baker gave **Shelley** an extra loaf of bread.
(*Shelley* is the indirect object to whom the loaf was given.)

Use your imagination to complete the sentences. Circle the indirect objects.

1. The lunch lady poured _____

2. The doctor told _____

3. The chef cooked _____

4. The lawyer gave _____

5. The mechanic promised _____

6. The carpenter built _____

7. The musician sang _____

8. The artist painted _____

9. The professor taught _____

10. The clerk sold _____

To Whom It May Concern

A **direct object** receives the action of an action verb. An **indirect object** is the person *for whom* or *to whom* something is done.

> **Example:** The artist sketched **me** a **picture**.
> (*Picture* is the direct object, and *me* is the indirect object for whom the picture was sketched.)

Underline the direct objects. Circle the indirect objects.

1. The genie granted me three wishes.

2. My grandmother baked Josh a birthday cake.

3. My sister told Derek an interesting story.

4. Sophie saved me some extra ketchup.

5. Aunt Linda mailed Susan an invitation.

6. Rosa gathered Mom some wildflowers.

7. Stephen planted Louisa some tomato plants.

8. The shortcut saved us some time.

9. Eliza saved me some patches for my pants.

10. The waiter is bringing us our dinner right now.

Point Out the Irregulars

Regular verbs are made past tense by adding an **ed.** The form of **irregular verbs** must change.

Write *regular* **(R)** or *irregular* **(I)** next to each verb below. Then write the past tense of the verb on the line.

1. see _____

2. eat _____

3. climb _____

4. fight _____

5. dive _____

6. compete _____

7. swing _____

8. wake _____

9. blow _____

10. reveal _____

11. scream _____

12. insist _____

13. whisper _____

14. begin _____

15. steal _____

16. shine _____

17. suggest _____

18. shake _____

19. defeat _____

20. avoid _____

Daily Skill-Builders Grammar & Usage 5–6
walch.com © 2004 Walch Publishing

Pick Out the Irregulars

A **regular verb** is made past tense by adding **ed.** The form of an **irregular verb** is changed when it is made past tense.

Write the past tense of each verb on the lines below. Draw a funny shape around each irregular verb.

1. burst

_____

2. ring

_____

3. observe

_____

4. force

_____

5. freeze

_____

6. disregard

_____

7. know

_____

8. bite

_____

9. wear

_____

10. demand

_____

11. effect

_____

12. sink

_____

13. hoist

_____

14. come

_____

15. hide

_____

Mixed-Up Verbs

A **singular subject** takes a **singular verb**. A **plural subject** takes a **plural verb**.

Examples: He **plays** soccer with Tim.
Hillary and Jessica **play** the flute.

The **bold** verbs below are in the wrong sentences. For each sentence, choose the correct verb from the other sentences and write it on the line. The first one has been done for you.

1. Jamie **mows** past Sam's Laundromat. _____walks_____

2. The girls on the team **grows** good pitches. _____

3. The big, brown cow **sit** on top of the hay. _____

4. Some children can't **sleeps** quietly for two hours. _____

5. The pizza **walks** like burnt tomatoes. _____

6. My neighbor **pick** chives and garlic in her garden. _____

7. Tortoises **glows** when they race hares. _____

8. My new watch **throw** in the dark. _____

9. They **smells** blueberries in the summer to make blueberry pie. _____

10. Ralph **lose** the neighbor's lawn every Sunday. _____

Mix and Match

A **singular subject** takes a **singular verb**. A **plural subject** takes a **plural verb**.

Match each subject below with a verb in the box. Then write a sentence using the subject and the verb.

skate	fly	melt	protects	races	slides
falls	hibernate	burns	hide	treat	bakes

1. bears _____

2. a skier _____

3. icicles _____

4. kids _____

5. doctors _____

6. fire _____

7. snow _____

8. birds _____

9. my grandmother _____

10. a snow fort _____

11. our car _____

12. mice _____

Reach an Agreement

A **singular subject** takes a **singular verb**. A **plural subject** takes a **plural verb**.

Fill in the lines below using the verbs from the box. Make sure the verbs agree with the subjects. Write two more sentences to conclude the story. Cross off the words as you use them.

buys	glows	want	comes	shine	are	is
love	gives	walks	think	glide	ride	use

1. Uncle Jeremy _____ us a gift each year.

2. My sisters and I _____ Uncle Jeremy _____ the best.

3. He always _____ to our birthday parties, even though we _____ older now.

4. He usually _____ us something we _____ at school.

5. Last year I got a backpack that _____ in the dark.

6. My sisters' backpacks don't _____ like mine.

7. This year, Uncle Jeremy bought us two skateboards that _____ very fast.

8. We _____ the skateboards, but there are three of us.

9. Shelley _____ to school, while Tracy and I _____ our bikes.

10. We all _____ to skateboard to school.

11. _____

12. _____

Daily Skill-Builders Grammar & Usage 5–6
walch.com © 2004 Walch Publishing

Tricky Transitives

A **transitive verb** is an action verb that is followed by a direct object.

> **Example:** Julia **hums** songs when she listens to the radio.
> (*Hums* is a transitive verb that is followed by the direct object songs.)

If a verb in **bold** below is a transitive verb, write a **T** next to the sentence and underline the direct object. If a verb in bold is not a transitive, write **NT** next to the sentence.

____ 1. Louise **caught** the fly ball that Casey hit.

____ 2. Mrs. Howe **watches** television in her basement.

____ 3. I usually **run** past Sherry's house.

____ 4. We carefully **stepped** over the rabbit's hole.

____ 5. I **take** pictures of the people in my family.

____ 6. Josephine always **swims** in the water at the beach.

____ 7. David **glued** his fingers together.

____ 8. Jerry **makes** excellent ice cream.

____ 9. My grandfather **sleeps** in his chair.

____ 10. My little cousins **race** everywhere at camp.

____ 11. We **snipped** the flowers before putting them in the vase.

____ 12. The governor **called** the winner to congratulate him.

____ 13. Do gorillas **eat** bananas, too?

____ 14. The rabbit **sprang** out of its hole.

____ 15. I've already **hung** the picture on my wall.

Make It Transitive

A **transitive verb** is an action verb that is followed by a direct object.

> **Example:** Jeremy **whispered** the secret to Bill.
> (*Whispered* is a transitive verb that is followed by the direct object *secret*.)

Make each underlined verb below a transitive verb by adding a direct object above the sentence. The first one has been done for you.

1. The bandleader <u>waved</u> ^his hand at the musicians to play softly.

2. The bandleader <u>conducts</u> very well.

3. The trumpet players <u>blew</u> into the saxophone players' ears.

4. The drummer <u>beat</u> very hard.

5. Sandra, the tuba player, <u>reads</u> very slowly.

6. The chorus sometimes <u>sings</u> with the band.

7. The soloist <u>performed</u> very well.

8. The audience enjoys <u>hearing</u>.

9. Sometimes parents <u>hum</u> when the band plays.

10. Two saxophone players also <u>play</u> in the jazz band.

11. The band <u>is practicing</u> every day until the concert.

12. Most players <u>carry</u> home after practice.

Daily Skill-Builders Grammar & Usage 5–6
walch.com © 2004 Walch Publishing

It All Ends Here

An **intransitive verb** is an action verb that does not have a direct object.

    Example: The boy **coughed** during the concert.
               (*Coughed* is the intransitive verb.)

Some verbs could be either transitive or intransitive verbs, depending on the sentence. Make the verbs below **intransitive verbs** by choosing the correct ending to the sentence. Circle the correct ending.

1. We dug
    a. holes on the farm.
    b. in our neighbor's garden.

2. We pushed
    a. past a large group of people.
    b. the car up the hill.

3. My brother delivers
    a. to every house in the neighborhood.
    b. the Sunday paper.

4. I can mash
    a. after I finish doing this.
    b. the potatoes for dinner.

5. We burst
    a. the bubble Maggie made.
    b. into the room.

6. We all shake
    a. orange juice before we drink it.
    b. when we dance.

7. I chew
    a. very slowly sometimes.
    b. my food with care.

8. I already ate
    a. a large hamburger with fries.
    b. before I came.

9. We hid
    a. the bracelet in the garden.
    b. under the bed.

10. We sank
    a. off the coast of Mexico.
    b. our boats in the bathtub.

Intransitive Verbs

An **intransitive verb** is an action verb that does not have a direct object. Although most verbs can be either transitive or intransitive, some verbs can only be intransitive because they do not take a direct object. Linking verbs are always intransitive.

Example: We **came** late to the party.

(It doesn't make sense to ask the question *who?* or *what?* after *came*.)

Circle the verbs below that (usually) do not take a direct object.

1. go	2. dive	3. shrink	4. rise
5. fall	6. draw	7. glide	8. twirl
9. laugh	10. slither	11. break	12. crawl

Choose five of the intransitive verbs above. Then use each verb in a sentence.

13. _____

14. _____

15. _____

16. _____

17. _____

Daily Skill-Builders Grammar & Usage 5–6
walch.com © 2004 Walch Publishing

On the Farm

A **transitive verb** is an action verb that is followed by a direct object. An **intransitive verb** is an action verb that does not have a direct object.

Write **T** next to the sentences below that contain transitive verbs. Circle the direct object. Write **I** next to the sentences that contain intransitive verbs.

____ 1. The farmer <u>milks</u> the cows early in the morning.

____ 2. The chickens <u>make</u> noise every time I come near them.

____ 3. Our clothes <u>fluttered</u> in the breeze on the clothesline.

____ 4. I <u>shoveled</u> a lot of dirt this afternoon.

____ 5. We <u>worked</u> until the sun went down.

____ 6. I <u>drove</u> a tractor for the first time.

____ 7. Mr. Hayes and the family <u>eat</u> in the dining room.

____ 8. The family <u>cooks</u> in a beautiful, old kitchen.

____ 9. The corn <u>grew</u> in our field.

____ 10. My sister helps <u>pick</u> the vegetables.

____ 11. The old barn may <u>collapse</u> soon.

____ 12. We will <u>build</u> a new barn in the summer.

____ 13. I <u>noticed</u> five new calves this year.

____ 14. The new calves <u>cling</u> to their mothers.

____ 15. I will <u>leave</u> the farm next year.

On to Adjectives

An **adjective** is a word that describes a noun or a pronoun.

Example: The water at the **sandy** beach was very **cold.**
(*Sandy* describes *beach* and *cold* describes *water.*)
She was very **smart.**
(*Smart* describes the pronoun *she.*)

Circle the adjectives in the sentences below. Underline the nouns they describe.

1. We brought a big bag of games.

2. Bears can be dangerous when protecting their cubs.

3. The kind gentleman returned my earring.

4. Sharks have large mouths!

5. The audience loved the talented dancer.

6. The fastest runner will win the prize.

7. We stayed at the best camp in the world.

8. The rare jewels are on display in the museum.

9. We bought beautiful flowers at the market.

10. The pavement is hot in the summer.

11. We don't like to ride the crowded subway.

12. The mason fixed the brick wall.

13. We should drive the new car.

14. We can see the bright stars in the sky.

15. Our tent is too small to take on the trip.

A Room of Adjectives

An **adjective** is a word that describes a noun or a pronoun. They tell *how many*, *what kind*, or *which one*.

Examples: We made **sixteen** sandwiches. **(How many?)**
Female birds lay eggs. **(What kind?)**
The **large** box is mine. **(Which one?)**

Underline the adjectives in the sentences below.

1. My brown jacket is in my closet.

2. My comfortable bed is against the wall.

3. The large windows let in lots of sunlight.

4. I sit on my comfortable chair when I read.

5. My carpet is white and gray.

6. I have a noisy bird in my room.

7. My new clock is next to my bed.

8. I have ten books on my shelf.

9. There is a tall mirror against the wall.

10. Harmless spiders hide under my desk.

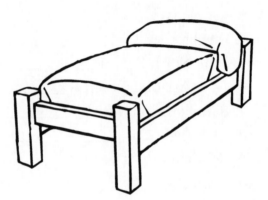

Adjectives That Compare

An **adjective** is a word that describes a noun or a pronoun. A **comparative adjective** compares two people, places, things or ideas.

> **Examples:** Your painting is **large**. (adjective)
> Your painting is **larger** than mine. (comparative adjective)

Write a comparative adjective on the lines below.

1. The Empire State Building is _____ than my house.
2. Sammy Sosa is a _____ baseball player than I am.
3. Our grass is _____ than the neighbor's grass.
4. My brother is _____ than I was at his age.
5. The North Pole is _____ than my town.
6. The Atlantic Ocean is _____ than my pool.
7. Charlotte's hair is _____ than Kendra's hair.
8. A large fire is _____ than a small fire.
9. Our motorboat is _____ than that sailboat.
10. Drums are _____ than flutes.

A **superlative adjective** compares three or more people, places, things, or ideas.

> **Example:** That is the **most creative** idea I've heard today.

Write a superlative adjective on the lines below.

11. You have the _____ pencil in the class.
12. The _____ player in the band is the one I can always hear.
13. I have the _____ room in the house.
14. That is the _____ bouquet of roses I have ever seen.
15. He is the _____ of the five brothers.
16. My doctor told me that I was the _____ of all his patients.
17. They sell the _____ vegetable burgers in town.
18. We rode the _____ ride at the amusement park.
19. I took out the _____ book in the library.
20. We had the _____ class in the history of the school.

Daily Skill-Builders Grammar & Usage 5–6
walch.com © 2004 Walch Publishing

Scrambled Adjectives

An **adjective** is a word that describes a noun or a pronoun.

Unscramble the **superlative** and **comparative adjectives** in the sentences below. Write the unscrambled adjectives on the lines.

1. Today will be the **tohstet** day of the year, so I'm wearing shorts. _____

2. Erin is **ratsfe** than Shannon, so she will probably win the race. _____

3. That mansion is the **gsebtig** house on the block. _____

4. The man on stilts is **reltla** than you. _____

5. I left my hat out in the rain, so it is **rtewte** than your hat. _____

6. The North Star looks like the **tgireshbt** star in the sky. _____

7. The chocolate pie is **rwtesee** than the lemon pie. _____

8. I am **rhgrieun** than you because I didn't have breakfast. _____

9. Of the three women, Julianne has the **srteded** hair. _____

10. The vegetables the farmer gave us are the **ehrfstes** you can find. _____

11. The circle I made is **orduren** than the one you made. _____

12. These chips are **eprrcsii** than those chips. _____

13. The feather is surely **ghlriet** than my book. _____

14. Your little brother is the **sutect** baby I have ever seen. _____

15. Lenny is the **htesrsot** boy in his class. _____

Adjective Articles

Use the **adjective article** *an* before words that begin with a vowel. Use the **adjective article** *a* before words that begin with a consonant.

Write the correct article on the lines below.

1. ____ pillow

2. ____ umbrella

3. ____ shoe

4. ____ horse

5. ____ octopus

6. ____ artist

7. ____ watch

8. ____ igloo

9. ____ reindeer

10. ____ eraser

11. ____ judge

12. ____ apple

Use the **adjective article** *the* to refer to a specific noun. Use *a* or *an* to refer to nonspecific nouns.

Write the correct article on the lines below.

13. ____ dinner you made last night was delicious.

14. I don't know what's playing, but I want to see ____ funny movie.

15. We rode ____ bus that Kerry drives.

16. I would like ____ largest scoop of ice cream that you can scoop, please.

17. I would love to see ____ smile on someone's face.

18. I want to visit ____ foreign country.

19. I will take ____ bus downtown sometime today.

20. I want to visit ____ countryside of Portugal.

Point to It

Use the **adjective article** *the* to refer to specific nouns. Use the **adjective articles** *a* and *an* to refer to nonspecific nouns.

Write the correct article on the lines. If you use the article **the,** draw an arrow to the noun the article describes.

1. My dad has ____ bunch of old records in the basement.

2. I would like ____ doughnut with rainbow sprinkles, please.

3. Can you build me ____ tree house with a ladder?

4. I am making ____ apple pie.

5. We are going to build ____ best sundial in the world!

6. I saw ____ dog you were telling me about.

7. ____ papers near the window will be blown away.

8. Some day I would like to go on ____ trip to the moon.

9. I want to live on ____ island somewhere in the Caribbean.

10. I read ____ last book he ever wrote.

11. I want to give my dad ____ hammer that he asked for.

12. He bought ____ assortment of things.

13. Can we have ____ kitten with the orange stripes?

14. There is ____ crumb on my pillow.

15. We would like to see ____ circus that is in town.

At the Carnival

An **adverb** describes a verb, an adjective, or another adverb.

Examples: I **slowly** walked across the street. (*Slowly* describes the verb *walked*.)
I received a **very** good grade. (*Very* describes the adjective *good*.)
We ate the dessert **too quickly.** (*Too* describes the adverb *quickly*.)

Underline the adverbs in the sentences below.

1. The band at the carnival played loudly.

2. We quickly ate our snow cones before they melted.

3. My dad and I happily watched the artist draw pictures.

4. The mime silently gestured to me.

5. My brothers and I waited eagerly for the magician's show.

6. A ladybug softly landed on my shoulder.

7. The sun shone brightly on the crowd.

8. We saw a tent accidentally collapse.

9. The woman secretly gave me extra fried dough.

10. We rarely saw an unhappy person.

11. A clown skillfully folded a balloon animal for me.

12. A man on stilts carefully walked through the crowd.

13. We held on tightly when we went on rides.

14. The children looked both ways and safely crossed the street.

15. We will surely return next year.

Daily Skill-Builders Grammar & Usage 5–6
walch.com © 2004 Walch Publishing

Adverb Olympics

An **adverb** is a word that describes a verb, an adjective, or another adverb. Some adverbs tell *when*, *how often*, or *how long* something happens.

Complete the sentences with adverbs from the box below.

last	first	frequently	rarely	sooner
daily	recently	briefly	quickly	previously
yesterday	usually	temporarily	instantly	yearly

1. The sprinters ran _____ earlier this morning.

2. The athletes must train _____ for this.

3. Johnson was in first place _____ before Henrick overtook him.

4. My favorite event will be _____ later this evening.

5. I wish that this were a _____ event.

6. Kittredge _____ broke his leg, so he couldn't race.

7. We are _____ able to see so many talented athletes in one place.

8. The sprinter _____ lost sight of the finish line.

9. The tennis match finished _____ than I thought.

10. The concerned distance runner _____ checks his watch.

11. The weight lifters are _____ large.

12. The swimmers swam _____, and the runners will run today.

13. The cyclist _____ trained in France before coming to the Olympics.

14. When we saw Gustav smile, we _____ knew he had won.

15. The fifty-meter dash ended _____.

To What Degree?

An **adverb** is a word that describes a verb, an adjective, or another adverb. Some adverbs tell *how much* or *how little*.

Underline the adverbs in the sentences below.

1. They were completely exhausted after the long bike ride.

2. My cousin was very upset that we left.

3. The old woman was extremely kind to us.

4. My grandfather is quite extraordinary.

5. The baby bird is too cute for words.

6. The unbelievably silly clown sat on me.

7. Those statues look amazingly real.

8. We were totally surprised to see you.

9. The chair is certainly broken.

10. That painting is surely expensive.

11. My dog is never mean to people.

12. Unfortunately, Steve is always late.

13. My brother is strong enough to carry it.

14. I am a little lazy today.

15. After two steaks, I am quite full.

Daily Skill-Builders Grammar & Usage 5–6
walch.com © 2004 Walch Publishing

Summer Camp

Underline the **adverbs** in the sentences below.

1. We always go to camp in the summer.

2. My brother, sister, and I quickly run from the car to the cabins when we arrive.

3. We usually arrive first.

4. Our parents stay briefly until the other kids arrive.

5. We are very happy because there will be more kids this year.

6. We all live in extremely small cabins.

7. We live near a brook and a large field.

8. We walk to the main cabin daily to eat our meals.

9. The food is quite delicious.

10. I often ask for a second helping of the main dish.

11. Sometimes we have chocolate cake for dessert.

12. Every camper eagerly waits for the time when he or she can swim.

13. The island camp is completely surrounded by water.

14. We never miss an opportunity to swim.

15. I am really excited to come back next year.

Out to Dinner

A **pronoun** is a word used in place of a noun. A **subject pronoun** is used as the subject of a sentence.

> **Singular:** I, you, he, she it
> **Plural:** we, you, they

Replace the **bold** nouns below with a subject pronoun. Write the pronoun above them.

1. **The Old Red Boat** is the restaurant that we went to last night for dinner.

2. **My grandparents** took us out to dinner.

3. **My parents, my brother, and I** all went together.

4. **My grandfather** was celebrating his sixtieth birthday.

5. **The food** was mainly seafood but very delicious.

6. **The waitress** was very kind to us.

7. **The restaurant** was a floating boat.

8. **My family and I** sat next to the window.

9. **Jackie (myself)** could see a dozen other boats.

10. **One boat** was directly across from where I was sitting.

11. **My father** ordered lobster, and as he was breaking off the tail something happened.

12. **The tail** broke off with a loud *snap!*

13. **My mother and I** noticed something happening outside at the other boat.

14. **The mast** of the ship broke in two!

15. Luckily, **the people** on board weren't hurt.

Daily Skill-Builders Grammar & Usage 5–6
walch.com © 2004 Walch Publishing

Subject Switch!

A **pronoun** is a word used in place of a noun. A **subject pronoun** is used as the subject of a sentence.

Cross out the **bold** pronoun in the sentence and replace it with the subject pronoun at the top of the box. If the verbs and the subject pronouns do not agree, correct the verb.

I	we
1. **We** went to the zoo with Tara and Lindsey.	3. **It** fell out of the canoe when Josh stood up.
2. **She** likes mint chocolate chip ice cream.	4. **She** brings him flowers in the hospital.

you (singular)	you (plural)
5. **Them** buys the red socks with the white stripes.	7. Do **they** like my posters?
6. **I** am building a sand castle with Donna.	8. **She** will love the five pounds of spaghetti I made.

she	They
9. **I** like to visit the dentist!	11. **It** is coming to my birthday party.
10. **They** raise beautiful monarch butterflies.	12. **She** fills up the auditorium.

A Trip to the Museum

A **pronoun** is a word used in place of a noun. An **object pronoun** is used as a direct object, an indirect object, or in a prepositional phrase.

> **Singular:** me, you, him, her, it
> **Plural:** us, you, them

Replace the noun (or nouns) in **bold** with an object pronoun. The first one has been done for you.

1. My mom, my dad, and I went with ~~my sister Joanna~~ to the museum. *(her)*

2. My family took **an umbrella** because it was raining out.

3. The museum had an exhibit on **Pablo Picasso.**

4. Picasso was a great painter who inspired **my family and me.**

5. "You should definitely see **the exhibit,**" our teacher told **Joanna.**

6. The paintings gave **the visitors** goosebumps because the paintings were so beautiful.

7. They didn't bring their favorite picture for **viewers** because the picture was in Paris.

8. "You should buy **Joanna** a postcard, Dad," Joanna said to her father.

9. It was difficult to see **the paintings** above the crowd.

10. My dad put **Joanna** on his shoulders to let **Joanna** see.

11. Joanna complained, "You're not lifting **Joanna** high enough, Dad."

12. Dad moved to another location for **Joanna.**

13. My mother gave **Joanna** the umbrella to hold.

14. As Dad was moving, I saw **the umbrella** slip out of Joanna's hand.

15. The umbrella hit **the painting** and knocked **the painting** to the ground!

Daily Skill-Builders Grammar & Usage 5–6
walch.com © 2004 Walch Publishing

Fill in the Objects

A **pronoun** is a word used in place of a noun. An **object pronoun** is used as a direct object, an indirect object, or in a prepositional phrase.

> **Singular:** me, you, him, her, it
> **Plural:** us, you, them

Write a sentence in each blank using the object pronouns given. The first one has been done for you.

me	us
1. Direct object: Please lead **me** to the manager.	3. Direct object: _____
2. Indirect object: _____	4. Indirect object: _____
you	**you**
5. Direct object: _____	7. Direct object: _____
6. Indirect object: _____	8. Indirect object: _____
him	**them**
9. Direct object: _____	11. Direct object: _____
10. Indirect object: _____	12. Indirect object: _____

Possessive Pronouns

A **possessive pronoun** shows ownership. It can stand alone or be used before a noun.

Examples: I rode **my** bike. (*My* comes before the noun *share*.)
The bike outside is **mine.** (*Mine* can stand alone.)

> **Before a noun:**
> my, your, his, her, its, our, their
> **Stand alone:**
> mine, yours, his, hers, its, ours, theirs

Complete the sentences below with the correct possessive pronoun.

1. Ted and his family love _____ gifts.

2. We all left _____ glasses by the sink.

3. I can't believe I lost _____ pink sunglasses!

4. Ted said that the shoes in the corner are _____.

5. You should have _____ hair cut very short.

6. They told me that the game was _____.

7. I lost a white sweatshirt, so that one must be _____.

8. The house lost _____ roof when the tornado ripped through town.

9. She wishes that the cat were _____ because she wants a pet.

10. It is _____ turn to go because he's next in line.

Daily Skill-Builders Grammar & Usage 5–6
walch.com © 2004 Walch Publishing

Reflexives in the Mirror

A **reflexive pronoun** refers back to the subject.

    Example: Juan enjoyed listening to **himself.**

Match the phrases on the left with the phrases on the right by drawing a line.

1. Jena always buys	themselves silly.
2. Mike likes to pat	himself to work in the morning.
3. Aisha and Kim laugh	myself that it will be okay.
4. We helped	herself gifts on vacation.
5. Malik drives	himself on the back after a good game.
6. I like to tell	ourselves to second helpings.
7. The dog licked	yourself a new partner.
8. They each gave	ourselves in danger.
9. You will have to find	itself before going to bed.
10. We accidentally put	themselves a bonus.

Possessive or Reflexive?

A **possessive pronoun** shows ownership. It can stand alone or be used before a noun. A **reflexive pronoun** refers back to the subject.

> **Examples:** We took **our** cat to the veterinarian. (*Our* is a possessive pronoun.)
>
> He looked at **himself** in the mirror. (*Himself* is a reflexive pronoun.)

Complete the sentences below with either a possessive or reflexive pronoun. Write a **P** in the blank next to each sentence for possessive pronouns. Write an **R** for reflexive pronouns.

_____ 1. I left my book here, so it must be _____.

_____ 2. He already took _____ share with him.

_____ 3. We bought _____ a new house last week.

_____ 4. The dog wagged _____ tail at the boy.

_____ 5. They have a red boat, so that boat is probably _____.

_____ 6. He treated _____ to a new pair of shoes.

_____ 7. She rubbed _____ hands with lotion.

_____ 8. They saw _____ in the store's mirror.

_____ 9. I saw that man with the bag, so it must be _____.

_____ 10. She made _____ a ham sandwich for lunch.

If a pronoun below is correct, leave it alone. If a pronoun is incorrect, cross it out and write in the correct pronoun.

11. The blue pens on the table are their.

12. We looked at ours in the pond's reflection.

13. He said that he had his camera with him.

14. The bike with the red stripe is mine.

15. He lost himself watch when he went swimming.

Daily Skill-Builders Grammar & Usage 5–6
walch.com © 2004 Walch Publishing

Me, Myself, and I

Use either a **possessive** or **reflexive pronoun** on the lines below.

Examples: Alicia wanted **her** camera. **(possessive)**
Alicia bought **herself** a new camera. **(reflexive)**

1. Timothy found the gloves, but I think _____ shoes are in the corner.

2. Sheila treated _____ to a large ice-cream sundae.

3. We all worked together, so the project is _____.

4. The fish in the pond made _____ way around the edge.

5. Mr. Jacobs taught _____ how to play the harmonica.

6. I saw Tyrone and Greg wearing the red jackets, so those must be _____.

7. I tell _____ that the spider won't bite me.

8. The dog wagged _____ tail when it saw the dog bone.

9. I want to wear _____ best outfit to dinner.

10. Rick and Jose stopped _____ before they interrupted the teacher.

11. This must be _____ because it is not mine.

12. Some animals build _____ new nests every day.

Find the Antecedent

An **antecedent** is the noun that a pronoun replaces or refers to.

> **Example:** My dad's **watch** works perfectly now that **it** has a new battery.
> (_Watch_ is the antecedent of the pronoun _it_.)

Draw an arrow from the pronoun in **bold** to its antecedent.

1. Artists painted many scenes when **they** had the time.

2. Our family brought coats because **we** thought that it would be cold.

3. Raspberries are especially delicious when **they** are on top of ice cream.

4. Natalia forgot that **she** had already signed the book.

5. Jack took one look and then **he** shut the door.

6. The house looks beautiful now that **it** is finished.

7. Andy told Terry, "**You** should bake these tonight."

8. When Rashid saw Janet crying, **he** comforted her.

9. The group will go if **we** can agree on a time.

10. The rabbit hopped out of its hole, and then **it** looked around.

Daily Skill-Builders Grammar & Usage 5–6
walch.com © 2004 Walch Publishing

Pronoun-Antecedent Match

An **antecedent** is the noun that a pronoun replaces or refers to.

> **Example:** That **chair** is broken, so you shouldn't sit on **it.**
> (*Chair* is the antecedent of the pronoun *it.*)

Fill in the missing pronouns below. Circle the pronoun's antecedent.

1. My bike works perfectly now that _____ is fixed.

2. My parents don't want to go because _____ don't like the opera.

3. Because Sharon and I don't like squid, _____ are not going to eat dinner.

4. Pedro, _____ should bring these binoculars to the lake.

5. Jill saw a moose, and _____ was frightened.

6. Anna doesn't like the beach, so _____ is staying at home.

7. Amanda and Joey, _____ should both be more careful with knives.

8. Manuel liked to cook, so _____ became a chef.

9. My friends wanted to see a movie, so _____ went to the movie theater.

10. The skateboard would work better if _____ had another wheel.

Arrows and Antecedents

An **antecedent** is the noun that a pronoun replaces or refers to.

Example: The **chairs** got wet when we left **them** in the rain.
(*Chairs* is the antecedent of the pronoun *them*.)

Draw a line connecting a pronoun with an antecedent. Write sentences below using the pairs you have made. Use each pronoun once. The first one has been done for you.

1.	the marine biologists	we
2.	Mr. Hammerstein	you (singular)
3.	Nicole	they
4.	my little sister and I	she
5.	the flight attendant	he
6.	the carpenters	you (plural)
7.	the waiter	them
8.	Ivan	her
9.	the band and I	him
10.	Jamal and Dale	us

1. The marine biologists said that they were going to the ocean today. _____

2. _____

3. _____

4. _____

5. _____

6. _____

7. _____

8. _____

9. _____

10. _____

Daily Skill-Builders Grammar & Usage 5–6
walch.com © 2004 Walch Publishing

A Few Indefinite Pronouns

An **indefinite pronoun** refers to people, places, or things in general—not specifically.

> **Some indefinite pronouns:** anyone, both, many, nobody, somebody

Underline the indefinite pronouns in the sentences below. Some of the sentences shouldn't have an indefinite pronoun. For those sentences, cross out the indefinite pronoun and fill in with another word (or words).

1. Nobody always buys two french rolls when he comes to visit.

2. Nothing is good enough for my favorite aunt.

3. Something rattles when the car goes over bumps.

4. Few of the customers like pistachio ice cream.

5. Everybody will never see our cousins in Ireland.

6. Several of the students are going on the field trip.

7. Both is going to be the best game ever!

8. Either of the two dresses would look pretty.

9. I saw somebody, the man with the red jacket, last night.

10. Much of the coastline is populated.

11. One will be plenty because the flavor is so strong.

12. Some would be better than none, I'd say.

13. Anybody like my neon yellow pants.

14. All was going well until I became sick.

15. I don't like the first or the second option, so neither sounds good to me.

It's All Relative

Relative pronouns connect words in one part of the sentence to another part of the sentence. They are used to introduce adjective clauses. Often, *who* is used for people, *which* for things, and *that* for people or things.

Example: The boy **who** ate five cheeseburgers will surely get sick.
(*Who ate five cheeseburgers* is an adjective clause that tells about the boy.)

Choose relative pronouns from the box to complete the sentences below. You will use some pronouns more than once.

who	whom	whose	which	what
that	whoever	whatever	whichever	

1. You should invite the person _____ manners are the best.

2. You gave the fish to _____ yesterday?

3. My brother will eat _____ is on the table.

4. Can you tell me _____ one Judy would like?

5. I saw the actor _____ starred in your movie.

6. My sister wants _____ piece is the largest.

7. The group _____ finishes first will receive the award.

8. Jerry, _____ brought the bread, will bring more tomorrow.

9. My mom buys _____ is on sale.

10. The teacher said, "_____ wants to come needs to take this bus."

11. I would like to have _____ I had yesterday.

12. Tania and Teresa want _____ drink is orange flavored.

13. Do you know _____ of the two drums Jake would like?

14. I don't know the person _____ car is parked outside.

15. I played the game _____ we saw advertised.

Daily Skill-Builders Grammar & Usage 5–6
walch.com © 2004 Walch Publishing

Conjunctions Make Sense!

Conjunctions connect individual words or groups of words.

> **Some conjunctions:** and, but, or, nor, for, so, yet

Each sentence below is missing one of the conjunctions listed above. Draw a caret (^) where the conjunction should be and write it above the sentence.

1. We like to dance sing in the rain.

2. My mother broke her leg, she is still in good spirits.

3. We could have our picnic on the hill at the park.

4. I didn't see him do I want to see him.

5. I got a card a new bike for my birthday.

6. We should take the clothes out of the rain, they will get wet.

7. We swam in the ocean, we built sand castles.

8. My father is away, you can't see him right now.

9. Ruby doesn't like to shop, she still comes with me to the mall.

10. I want to see my cousin in Texas, I am going there next week.

Conjunction Pair-Up

A **conjunction** connects words or phrases. Some conjunctions are used in pairs.

Some conjunctions used in pairs: either/or, neither/nor, not only/ but/also, both/and, whether/or, as/so

Complete the sentences below with a pair of conjunctions listed above.

1. _____ wind _____ ice will stop me from skiing today.

2. _____ Juan _____ Jeff are staying at the lodge.

3. _____ you like it _____ not, you have to finish your homework.

4. _____ long as I am living here, _____ should you.

5. _____ have the birds left the nest, _____ they have _____ flown south.

6. _____ we are taking the train, _____ we are walking fifty blocks.

7. _____ sunscreen _____ a bathing suit are essential at the beach.

8. _____ a green dragon _____ a blue monkey is under your bed.

9. _____ has Nicole eaten all of the cake, _____ she has _____ taken the ice cream.

10. _____ the rabbit did it _____ not, some critter dug a hole in my yard.

Daily Skill-Builders Grammar & Usage 5–6
walch.com © 2004 Walch Publishing

Catch a Dependent Clause

Conjunctions connect words or phrases. A **subordinating conjunction** introduces a dependent clause.

Example: We lost our way **when** the blizzard came. **(subordinating conjunction)**

Draw lines to connect a word or phrase from each column to make a sentence. The first one has been done for you. Write the sentences at the bottom of the page.

1.	We took a boat to the island	when	she has her pacifier.
2.	I have to take my medicine	unless	I ate dinner.
3.	I get nervous	where	I turned it off.
4.	The baby will cry	before	my body heals.
5.	I found my shoes	because	I fly on planes.
6.	I went swimming	so that	my visit last October.
7.	My sister chews gum	as though	we can't swim.
8.	The little drummer acts	so	I left them.
9.	I haven't seen the ocean	while	he was in a band.
10.	The music was hurting my head,	since	she talks on the phone.

1. We took a boat to the island because we can't swim. _____

2. _____

3. _____

4. _____

5. _____

6. _____

7. _____

8. _____

9. _____

10. _____

Inject Life in These Sentences!

Interjections are words or phrases that express strong emotions. Use commas and exclamation points to set them apart from the rest of the sentence.

Use the interjections in the box to add some emotion to the sentences below. Add punctuation where needed. The first one has been done for you.

fantastic	ouch	yum	that's terrible	wait
well	terrific	wow	unbelievable	look
hey	gosh	great	sorry	oh no

1. Wow! Those monkeys are blue and green.

2. There's a brick falling from the sky.

3. That crab's claws can really hurt.

4. I didn't think that vegetable pie would taste good.

5. I am so happy that all of my friends will be there.

6. Maybe we will have better luck the next time we run.

7. Banana ice cream is my favorite.

8. I think that Brian took Sanjay's jacket.

9. That's my book you're taking.

10. Those snakes are long.

11. I am so glad that we're going to the circus.

12. You can't leave without saying good-bye.

13. I can't believe he lost all of it.

14. I didn't mean to spill that on you.

15. You will love London.

Create the Mood

Interjections are words or phrases that express strong emotions. Use commas and exclamation points to set them apart from the rest of the sentence.

Put an interjection before each of the sentences below. Choose any interjection and use correct punctuation.

gosh	excellent	wow	oh no	super
ouch	watch out	look	wait	fantastic
hey	that's terrible	great	sorry	look out

1. The puddle outside is growing into a lake.

2. I found a piece of chocolate in my strawberry pie.

3. The paper you wrote was excellent.

4. The boys next door are coming with us.

5. He may try to convince you, too.

6. I have read four books this week.

7. We're moving away next month.

8. I just fell on the ice outside.

9. There are three bands playing tonight.

10. I will get the mop to clean that up.

11. We are going to sing in the concert tonight.

12. I forgot my homework.

13. There are a lot of people here.

14. We are going to watch four movies tonight.

15. There is a giant bee flying around you.

A Picture's Worth 1,000 Words

Prepositions show position or direction.

    Example: We slid the paper **underneath** the door.

Describe the scene below using prepositions. The first one has been done for you.

1.   The balloon glided through the clouds. _____

2.   _____

3.   _____

4.   _____

5.   _____

6.   _____

7.   _____

8.   _____

9.   _____

10.   _____

Position the Players

Prepositions show position or direction.

Use the prepositions in the box to complete the sentences below.

behind	under	inside	over	at
past	into	beside	on	near
through	toward	of	between	across

1. The goalie should stand _____ the goal.

2. Someone needs to kick the ball _____ net for the goal.

3. You should hit the ball with the front _____ your head.

4. Neil should run _____ the goal.

5. Debra should get _____ the player that she is blocking.

6. Be careful not to roll _____ the ball.

7. Don't put your hands _____ the ball.

8. Aim the ball _____ the posts of the net.

9. Try to kick the ball _____ the other team's goalie.

10. Don't aim the ball _____ another player.

11. Stay _____ the boundary lines.

12. You can kick the ball _____ the other players' heads.

13. The ball won't go _____ the net.

14. Gloria should kick the ball _____ the field.

15. Don't stand directly _____ the goal for the entire game.

Nouns by Number

Fill in the missing **nouns** in the spaces below.

1 = common noun	**2** = proper noun	**3** = collective noun
4 = possessive noun	**5** = noun abbreviation	

1. I went to the _____ this past Saturday.
   2

2. It was on Park _____, which is near where my grandmother lives.
   5

3. There was a lot of music at the fair, and also a lot of _____.
   1

4. We saw a _____ of cows and a _____ of birds.
   3   3

5. My _____ quilts were on sale in the craft tent.
   4

6. We saw many crafts for sale, including _____ and _____.
   1   1

7. A lot of family friends were there, including Joe Reynolds, _____.
   5

8. _____ Marshall, our family doctor, volunteered for the dunk tank.
   5

9. _____ Marshall's sons took turns buying _____ to dunk
   5   1
   their mother.

10. My _____ favorite part of the fair was the pie-eating contest.
    4

11. The pies were from _____, which is in the next town.
    2

12. They were selling flowers, so I bought a _____ for my mother.
    3

13. My _____ flowers came from _____, which is a local florist.
    4   2

14. I had my face painted by a(n) _____ named _____.
    1   2

15. _____ painted _____ on my face. It was fun.
    2   1

Daily Skill-Builders Grammar & Usage 5–6
walch.com © 2004 Walch Publishing

Test Your Noun Skills

Label each underlined **noun** below as common (**C**), proper (**P**), collective (**CO**), possessive (**PO**), or abbreviation (**A**).

_____ **1.** Julie and <u>Margaret's</u> room is at the back of the house.

_____ **2.** We made a big <u>batch</u> of cookies for the bake sale on Friday.

_____ **3.** I had a <u>sandwich</u> and an <u>apple</u> for lunch.

_____ **4.** We will ride over the <u>Rocky Mountains</u> on our way to California.

_____ **5.** I saw a <u>gaggle</u> of geese fly over our heads.

_____ **6.** Maybe we should buy <u>Gerry's Old-Fashioned Ice Cream</u>.

_____ **7.** I have my <u>dad's</u> watch.

_____ **8.** The sign outside his office said Ted Li, <u>Ph.D.</u>

_____ **9.** Maybe I will ride my bike down Stephen's <u>Ave.</u>

_____ **10.** There is a <u>grove</u> of trees in back of the woodshed.

Make each underlined noun below plural.

11. The firefighters' <u>wife</u> knit warm winter <u>scarf</u>.

12. The <u>child</u> play in the playground after school.

13. Sometimes we see <u>deer</u> and <u>mouse</u> around our house.

14. A lot of ships come to the <u>wharf</u>.

15. All of these <u>chair</u> need to go in front of the <u>table</u>.

16. We ate roasted <u>potato</u> with our meal.

17. I will swim in many <u>pool</u> this summer.

18. There are many art <u>studio</u> near where I live.

19. The two <u>team</u> will be playing against each other tomorrow.

20. They say that cats have nine <u>life</u>.

Verse Yourself in Verbs

Label each underlined **verb** below as action **(A)**, helping **(H)**, or linking **(L)**.

_____ 1. The police officer <u>drove</u> right past us.

_____ 2. Those steaks <u>seem</u> a little burnt.

_____ 3. Your new bike <u>looks</u> very shiny.

_____ 4. Doris <u>has been</u> writing for a long time.

_____ 5. The dog <u>caught</u> the ball in his teeth.

_____ 6. The rabbit's ears <u>are</u> quite floppy.

_____ 7. You <u>must</u> help me lift this table.

_____ 8. We all <u>sing</u> in the choir.

_____ 9. You <u>are</u> very kind to him.

_____ 10. You <u>could</u> bring these papers to Sandy.

Label each underlined **verb** as transitive **(T)** or intransitive **(I)**.

_____ 11. The little boy <u>hopped</u> over the puddles.

_____ 12. We often <u>drink</u> soda at birthday parties.

_____ 13. I <u>won</u> a two-wheel bike in the raffle.

_____ 14. A few leaves <u>dropped</u> to the ground.

_____ 15. I <u>like</u> the magazines at the dentist's office.

Verbs to the Test

Underline the **direct objects** and circle the **indirect objects** in the sentences below.

1. We gave the charity fifty dollars.

2. They sent us chocolates in a box.

3. I sent him a beautiful postcard.

4. I brought the neighbors some homemade brownies.

5. The little boy blew the little girl a kiss.

Label the underlined **verbs** below as regular **(R)** or irregular **(I)**.

____ 6. The dogs <u>swim</u> all the way to the island.

____ 7. The mole always <u>digs</u> a hole in our backyard.

____ 8. I can <u>carry</u> those books for you.

____ 9. The man who comes from Holland <u>speaks</u> clearly.

____ 10. We <u>sift</u> through the sand looking for seashells.

Fill in the appropriate **tense**.

11. We _____ (past tense of *to ship*) my brother in college some chocolate chip cookies.

12. I _____ (future tense of *to sing*) in the concert tomorrow.

13. Maybe Mike and Tom _____ (past tense of *to sit*) on your papers.

14. Rubin usually _____ (present tense of *to play*) baseball in the park with his father.

15. My dad _____ (present tense of *to cook*) eggs and bacon every morning.

What Is Being Described?

An **adverb** describes a verb, an adjective, or another adverb. An **adjective** describes a noun or a pronoun.

Circle the descriptive adjectives below. Underline the adverbs. Draw an arrow from the adverb or adjective to the word that it describes.

1. We quickly walked across the busy street.

2. My mother and father are very nice people.

3. He is shy when he is meeting new people.

4. That is sweet tea.

5. We quickly skated over to the edge of the pond.

6. I love having a large room.

7. Your dress is a beautiful shade of pink.

8. We brought the crooked one home to show Mom.

9. I completely forgot to pass in my homework paper.

10. The bright, new lamp works perfectly.

11. Maybe his bravery will win him a gold medal.

12. The burrito is too large to eat with my hands.

13. The alarm buzzes softly in the morning.

14. I am thirsty after eating salty potato chips.

15. Martha hurriedly ran to meet her father.

Pronoun Review

Underline the **pronouns** below. Label each pronoun as subject, object, possessive, reflexive, indefinite, or relative.

_____ 1. We often listen to music while riding in the car.

_____ 2. The idea for the short story was mine.

_____ 3. Any student who wants to go on the field trip should sign up now.

_____ 4. Nobody wants to eat stale bread.

_____ 5. The three brothers gave themselves three gold stars.

_____ 6. Mrs. Ruby gave us chocolate for the holiday.

_____ 7. His shoes are very shiny.

_____ 8. Someone should help Mrs. Wilkinson with the groceries.

_____ 9. You should look for the rare birds.

_____ 10. Tania and Ray wrote a funny story for me.

_____ 11. The blue backpacks in the corner are theirs.

_____ 12. My aunt who gave me the skateboard is very nice.

_____ 13. Most like to watch the game on television.

_____ 14. Mrs. Chao wants to see our drawings on display.

_____ 15. Jimmy taught himself how to play the guitar.

Look! Review Parts of Speech!

Write either a **conjunction** or an **interjection** on the lines below.

1. _____! Those thorns are really sharp!

2. We watered the flowers, _____ then we mowed the grass.

3. _____ wind _____ rain will prevent us from going.

4. We could watch the moose, _____ we could go to the monkeys' cage.

5. _____, those flowers look so real!

6. _____, watch where you're going!

7. We stayed inside, _____ we wouldn't get wet during the storm.

8. _____ April _____ Bessie are going away this weekend.

9. I want to play a video game, _____ then I want to see a movie.

10. _____, there are four ladybugs on my hand!

Underline the **prepositions** in the sentences below.

11. We all ran under the tent when it started raining.

12. I left my jacket inside the house.

13. My little brother poured sand on my shoes.

14. We threw the garbage down the chute.

15. We walked toward the sound of laughter.

Memorial Day

Always **capitalize** the first word of a sentence. Capitalize days of the week, months of the year, and holidays.

Capitalize the proper words in the sentences below. Write two sentences to complete the story.

Holiday Parade

we had a parade yesterday in front of the capitol building. it was a cloudy monday afternoon in may, but we didn't cancel the parade. every monday they sell vegetables and crafts near the capitol building. there were many people there for the fair and even more people for the parade.

we were celebrating memorial day. memorial day is a special holiday. parades are popular for memorial day, but not for such holidays as easter and christmas. memorial day is always observed on a monday. sometimes the official day is on a saturday, tuesday, or thursday. i like that i don't have to go to school on a monday. it is a nice break before the last day of school in june.

there were lots of floats and some people walking around on stilts. there were also clowns making balloons and people throwing candy at the crowd. the weather was hot like a warm summer day in july.

the next parade will be for the fourth of july, and i want to be a part of that one. it will be the saturday after my birthday and i can't wait!

_____

_____

_____

_____

_____

Capitalize Correctly

Capitalize days of the week, months of the year, and holidays.

Rewrite each word on the line with the correct capital letters.

1. wednesday _____

2. kwanza _____

3. holiday _____

4. christmas _____

5. july _____

6. months _____

7. december _____

8. hanukkah _____

9. monday _____

10. birthday _____

11. valentine's day _____

12. april _____

13. reunion _____

14. st. patrick's day _____

15. january _____

16. tuesday _____

A Proper Noun Picnic

A **proper noun** names a specific person, place, thing, or idea. It is always capitalized.

Example: Albert Einstein, Toronto, <u>The Biography of Sammy Tyler</u>, Christianity

Capitalize the proper nouns in the sentences below.

1. We went to fort dixon park for a picnic last saturday.

2. The park is near lake higgins, which is not far from lake magnum.

3. My favorite park is central park in new york city, new york.

4. There are also some very nice parks in san francisco and quebec city, too.

5. I went on a picnic with aunt harriet and my friend jordan.

6. jordan's little brother harry was going to come, but his mom wouldn't let him.

7. We brought lots of food from sam's deli.

8. I brought my favorite book, called <u>the adventures of silly sue</u>.

9. Jordan brought his favorite CD, called <u>walking on the clouds</u>.

10. We read books, listened to music, and gazed at mount fairfield in the distance.

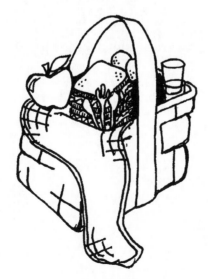

Which Ones Don't Belong?

A **proper noun** names a specific person, place, thing, or idea. It is always capitalized.

All of the nouns (including proper nouns) in the sentences below are capitalized. Cross out the first letter of the nouns that should **not** be capitalized.

1. Tracy and Nick took a Walk to Harmon's Flower Shop where they bought a Bouquet.

2. They bought some Daisies and Lilies to bring to Brenda's House.

3. After the flower Shop, they went to the Market.

4. They bought Meat at Darrel's Deli and Squash at Max's Farm Stand.

5. Everything was given to their Friend Brenda who is sick.

6. Brenda was at Dade County Hospital getting her Tonsils removed.

7. They wanted to make her Throat feel better, so they bought Ice Cream.

8. They had to get the good Kind of Ice Cream, so they went to Gus's Dairy Stand.

9. Once they had all of the Groceries, they walked to High Street.

10. They knocked on Brenda's Door and surprised her.

My Uncle Max

Capitalize the names of continents, countries, states and provinces, cities, and counties.

Identify the proper nouns that are not capitalized in the sentences below. Write the words correctly above the proper nouns.

1. Uncle Max went to europe last week to visit his friend in paris, france.

2. Uncle Max has been to many countries, such as china and spain.

3. He went to hong kong and beijing in china and to barcelona, spain.

4. He has been to all of the continents except africa.

5. Uncle Max liked asia the best, but australia was beautiful, too.

6. He has brought me back many gifts, including wooden shoes from norway and chopsticks from japan.

7. I have eaten peaches from georgia, lobster from maine, and potatoes from idaho, all because of Uncle Max.

8. I've seen pictures of canada from the provinces of british columbia to quebec.

9. My parents won't let me leave north america, so I will hope to go to miami, toronto, and chicago with Uncle Max.

10. Until then, I will live in detroit and visit Uncle Max at his home in houston, texas.

Pack Your Bags!

Capitalize the names of planets, continents, countries, states and provinces, cities, and counties.

Think of three items for each group below and list them. Don't forget to capitalize!

planets

1. _____

2. _____

3. _____

continents

4. _____

5. _____

6. _____

countries

7. _____

8. _____

9. _____

states and provinces

10. _____

11. _____

12. _____

cities

13. _____

14. _____

15. _____

counties

16. _____

17. _____

18. _____

Daily Skill-Builders Grammar & Usage 5–6
walch.com © 2004 Walch Publishing

Family Tree

Capitalize words such as *father* and *aunt* when the words are used as names.

Examples: I heard **Uncle** say that he was going to Florida tomorrow.
(*Uncle* is capitalized because it is used as a name. You could replace *Uncle* with his name.)
My **uncle** likes to travel.
(*Uncle* is not capitalized because it is not used as a name.)

For each relative below, write one sentence that uses the word as a name and one sentence that doesn't.

mother

1. _____

2. _____

father

3. _____

4. _____

aunt

5. _____

6. _____

uncle

7. _____

8. _____

grandfather

9. _____

10. _____

grandmother

11. _____

12. _____

Cap It!

Capitalize the words below that need to be capitalized.

1. i am going to sante fe, new mexico, with father and mother tomorrow.

2. we ate lunch with uncle luke at a little café in paris.

3. the best place to go in asia would be either china or japan.

4. my grandfather and i took interstate 45 to yellowstone national park.

5. many people fly during christmas and thanksgiving vacations.

6. if valentine's day is on a friday this year, my father will take mother on a trip.

7. we are going to sail on the pacific ocean for the whole month of may and a part of june.

8. i told uncle malcolm not to expect us at his home for kwanza this year.

9. maybe I will go to mars or pluto when I'm older.

10. grandfather rivera took us to the museum of natural history in new york city.

11. we drove across the rocky mountains on our way to moab, utah.

12. my sister and I saw the great barrier reef with our father.

13. next monday we should take a trip across the green mountains in vermont.

14. if mom would let me, I'd eat chocolate ice cream every friday, saturday, and sunday.

15. our whole family is going to be in ireland on st. patrick's day.

Daily Skill-Builders Grammar & Usage 5–6
walch.com © 2004 Walch Publishing

Family Reunion

Use a **period** after statements, commands, and requests.

> **Examples:** Sonia won the race. **(statement)**
> Bring the red paper. **(command)**
> Please pass the salsa. **(request)**

Trevor is having a family reunion. He has statements, commands, and requests to make. Place a period after the sentences below that need them. Label each of those sentences, telling if the sentence is a statement **(S),** a command **(C),** or a request **(R).** Leave the other sentences blank. Write one statement, one command, and one request at the bottom of the page.

1. Your mother tells me that you are playing sports in school, Trevor _____

2. Yes, I will you tell you about it, but first, please pass the ketchup _____

3. There is the ketchup _____

4. I am playing baseball and soccer _____

5. Do you like to play those sports _____

6. Yes, because the players on both teams are very nice _____

7. Use your father's glove for baseball _____

8. It would help if you could please bring Dad's glove the next time _____

9. Please remind me later _____

10. Will you come to my games _____

11. Tell me when the games are played _____

12. The first game is on April 10 _____

13. _____ R

14. _____ C

15. _____ S

A Trip to the Moon

Use a **question mark** after direct questions and when expressing doubt or requesting to make clear whether something is correct.

Examples: Do you want to ride next to me on the plane?
The auditorium can hold 1,800 (?) people.

Place a question mark in the correct places below. Place a period at the end of the other sentences. Then write five more sentences that ask questions at the bottom of the page.

1. Are there any mountains on the moon

2. I wonder what Earth looks like from the moon

3. Can you run on the moon

4. What color is the ground

5. One square mile on the moon has 500 craters, I think

6. If you'd like, I'll buy you a moon rock

7. Will I be able to go to the moon when I am older

8. Other solar systems have moons, too, right

9. I wonder if people will ever live on the moon

10. Would you go to the moon if you could

11. _____

12. _____

13. _____

14. _____

15. _____

Daily Skill-Builders Grammar & Usage 5–6
walch.com © 2004 Walch Publishing

Famous Author Interview

Use **questions marks** after direct questions and to express doubt about whether something is correct.

Imagine that you are meeting your favorite author. Write **eight direct questions** and **two statements that express doubt.**

Famous Author: _____

1. _____

2. _____

3. _____

4. _____

5. _____

6. _____

7. _____

8. _____

9. _____

10. _____

Jazz Them Up!

Use an **exclamation point** to express surprise or strong feelings. Use it after a word, a phrase, or a sentence.

Examples: Wait! **(word)**

Happy Birthday! **(phrase)**

I can't believe that we're going! **(sentence)**

Write an exclamation point after the words, phrases, and sentences that need one.

1. Hurry

2. Good job

3. Oranges are good for you

4. Look

5. Excellent idea

6. Follow the rules

7. Happy Anniversary

8. I love this

9. Please bring this with you

10. This is the best place in the world

11. Congratulations

12. You look fantastic

Think of four other words, phrases, or sentences that use an exclamation point and write them on the lines below.

13. _____

14. _____

15. _____

16. _____

Sweet Tooth!

Use an **exclamation point** to express surprise or strong feelings. Use it after a word, a phrase, or a sentence.

Imagine that your house is made of candy! You have a licorice bed, chocolate walls, and a gumdrop floor. Write twelve words, phrases, and sentences that express your surprise and excitement.

1. _____

2. _____

3. _____

4. _____

5. _____

6. _____

7. _____

8. _____

9. _____

10. _____

11. _____

12. _____

A Day at the Fair

Use an **exclamation point** to show surprise or strong feelings. Use a **period** after a sentence that is a statement, a command, or a request.

Lucas loves going to his school fair, but he only likes the pony rides and the cotton candy. Write an exclamation point after the sentences that convey Lucas's excitement or surprise. Write a period after the other sentences.

1. Look at the ponies

2. I am going to take four pony rides today

3. The ponies are so beautiful

4. I can't wait to ride

5. I will have to visit some other booths with my little brother

6. We will go to the dunk tank twice

7. We will eat hot dogs and popcorn

8. The cotton candy is delicious

9. I love the way it melts in my mouth

10. The popcorn sticks in my teeth

11. We have to finish eating before we ride the ponies

12. Maybe some day I will have my own pony

13. My brother Henry wants a rabbit instead

14. A pony would be the best gift in the world

15. I can't wait to come back to the fair next year

Make a Series!

Use **commas** between words or phrases in a series.

> **Examples:** My new bike is red**,** yellow**,** and green.
>
> I like to read books**,** play games**,** and build sand castles.

Write a series of at least three words or phrases to complete each sentence below.

1. My dog likes to _____

2. My favorite fruits are _____

3. When we go to the beach, we _____

4. In the winter, I like to _____

5. A fisherman may catch _____

6. A construction worker builds _____

7. Under my bed, you may find _____

8. The things I need the most are _____

9. A farmer might raise _____

10. My favorite cities are _____

Can You Switch Them?

Use a **comma** to separate adjectives that equally describe a noun. You can check if the adjectives are equal by switching their order.

Examples: I ate a cold ham sandwich for lunch.
(*Ham cold sandwich* doesn't sound correct, so don't place a comma between the adjectives.)
I ate a sticky, sandy sandwich at the beach.
(*Sandy, sticky sandwich* sounds correct, so use a comma.)

Place commas between the correct items below.

1. The large colonial house at the end of the road is mine.

2. Sandy and Teresa will bring their large pink backpacks.

3. Mike likes to take long boring drives through the mountains.

4. My family had big juicy burgers for dinner.

5. The gardener planted fragrant red flowers around the house.

6. The long fiction book you gave me was terrific!

7. The sticky squishy strawberry syrup is making a mess!

8. Please take my annoying baby brother with you.

9. The loud shiny trumpets were my favorite.

10. The hot summer sun was too bright to look at.

11. The nice substitute teacher let us go outside for recess.

12. He is the captain of a big red fishing boat.

13. It was a windy bitter raw day.

14. The cute little robin sings to me every morning.

15. I don't know anyone who dislikes gooey chocolate brownies.

Daily Skill-Builders Grammar & Usage 5–6
walch.com © 2004 Walch Publishing

Say It Again!

Use a **comma** to set off an appositive. An **appositive** is a word or phrase that renames the noun or pronoun that comes before it.

Example: My aunt, **the best nurse at the hospital,** works very hard.

For each sentence below, place commas around the appositives. Write two additional sentences that include appositives.

1. My brother the best player on the team received the award.

2. My aunt a great cook makes the best quesadillas in town.

3. Mrs. Hutchins a new teacher didn't know where to take the class.

4. We went to Fort Laramie Park my favorite park for a picnic lunch.

5. We took a train the Pacific Railroad to Mexico.

6. My rabbit the highest jumper in the East always escapes from its cage.

7. We love to eat chocolate-covered strawberries our favorite dessert on hot summer days.

8. Joe lives on Scammon Street a quiet side street with his three best friends.

9. Nick a very funny guy keeps us laughing all day long.

10. Mr. Ortega our neighbor across the street always says hello.

11. Coach Greely the girls' soccer coach is a very strict man.

12. We are going to Santigula a small island for vacation.

13. I want some papaya a tropical fruit for breakfast.

14.  _____

15. _____

Sentence Workout

Use **commas** in compound sentences. A **compound sentence** is made up of a coordinating conjunction (**and, but, or, nor, for, so,** and **yet**) and two clauses that can stand by themselves.

> **Example:** My mother loves plants, **so** we gave her one for her birthday.

Use a coordinating conjunction to complete each sentence below. If you form a compound sentence, write a comma before the conjunction.

1. He ran forty miles _____ he is very tired.

2. We could go to the movie theater _____ we could rent a DVD and stay at home.

3. I ate fifty chocolate pieces _____ then I felt really sick.

4. I like to look at squid in the aquarium _____ I don't want to eat one for dinner.

5. We went to the mall _____ the grocery store after dinner.

6. We will go to either Sam's camp _____ Hiroshi's house.

7. I have never seen a rattlesnake _____ do I want to see one.

8. My grandmother has a house on the beach _____ she goes there for the summer.

9. We will eat spinach _____ we will love it.

10. He remembered to lock the house _____ forgot to bring the key.

Daily Skill-Builders Grammar & Usage 5–6
walch.com © 2004 Walch Publishing

The Three C Rule

Use **commas** after **coordinating conjunctions** in **compound** sentences. A compound sentence is made up of a coordinating conjunction (**and, but, for, or, nor, so,** and **yet**) and two clauses that can stand alone as sentences.

Example: We broke the dishes, and then we glued them together.

Place a comma in each compound sentence below.

1. My mother broke her ankle so she is on crutches.

2. The paper flew off the desk and landed on the counter.

3. We will finish cooking but we can't do the dishes.

4. Kevin drove a bumper car and then he rode the roller coaster.

5. We will go to either Alaska or Mexico for vacation.

6. I have never been camping nor do I want to go camping.

7. We should bring our umbrellas for we will get wet if it rains.

8. The tickets will be sold quickly so come early.

9. My father complains about shoveling yet he refuses to let me help.

10. We may be there tomorrow but maybe not.

Commas are placed after the clauses in the beginning of the compound sentences below. Complete the sentences.

11. We would like to go, but _____

12. I will eat cake on my birthday, and then _____

13. Anthony forgot to bring his backpack to school, so _____

14. I will either play soccer this year, or _____

15. She didn't win first place, nor _____

Yes, No, and Well

Use a **comma** after *yes*, *no*, and *well* when these words appear at the beginning of a sentence.

Place a comma after *yes*, *no*, and *well* in the following sentences where necessary.

1. Janet said, "Well maybe it wouldn't be such a great idea."

2. I am feeling well today.

3. No I don't think we should swim after eating.

4. My mom always says "no" when I ask if I can play inside.

5. There are no raisins in my lunch box today.

6. Yes we should definitely bring sunscreen to the beach.

7. Well it would be easier to go if we had a ride.

8. I answered "yes" to all of the questions.

9. No maybe Grandpa isn't feeling well today.

10. Yes I would love to come with you.

Now write three sentences using *yes*, *no*, and *well*.

11. _____

12. _____

13. _____

Daily Skill-Builders Grammar & Usage 5–6
walch.com © 2004 Walch Publishing

Places, Everyone!

Use a **comma** to separate the name of someone you are directly addressing from the rest of the sentence.

Example: Please, Sharon, leave Tania's pigtails alone.

Imagine that you are directing your friends in a play. Write ten sentences addressing your friends.

1. _____

2. _____

3. _____

4. _____

5. _____

6. _____

7. _____

8. _____

9. _____

10. _____

Give Me a Break!

Use a **comma** after long prepositional phrases that appear at the beginning of a sentence.

> **Example:** After leaving my house this morning, I realized that I had forgotten a pencil.

Underline the prepositional phrases in the sentences below. If the phrase appears at the beginning of the sentence, use a comma after it.

1. Before the storm I was playing with my dog.

2. With this degree of confusion I'll buy a map.

3. I ate two hot dogs during the baseball game.

4. Until the end of the storm no one can say a word.

5. The fox ran in front of the bike.

6. I put all of my notebooks on my desk.

7. Except for the last three words I memorized the entire poem.

8. I found a rabbit's hole beside the tree in the backyard.

9. Without my science notes I couldn't do my homework.

10. Up to the last month of school I had never missed a day.

Write a long prepositional phrase, followed by a comma, on the lines below.

11. Before _____ the famous actor was a waiter in New York.

12. After _____ I got an ice-cream headache.

13. Besides _____ he is also a well-known photographer.

14. Except for _____ I have never seen a zebra.

Daily Skill-Builders Grammar & Usage 5–6
walch.com © 2004 Walch Publishing

Catch a Breath!

Commas can be used to tell the reader where to pause. In the sentences below, tell the reader where to pause by filling in the missing commas.

1. I had bacon tomatoes turkey onions and cucumbers in my salad.

2. If you go to the mall would you buy me a CD?

3. We could buy Mom a gift or we could make her one.

4. Keisha would you please come over here?

5. Yes I should have thought of that before.

6. My grandfather who was a captain on a fishing boat loves the ocean.

7. I like your bright shiny bracelet.

8. The frog jumped onto the lily pad and it caught a fly.

9. Jerry toss the ball to Patrick next time.

10. My favorite book the one that you lent to me is lost.

11. We packed lunches put the boat on the car and drove to the lake.

12. I don't like that slimy sticky thing on my plate.

13. Well maybe I should bring the clothes inside.

14. Mr. Kim may we please go outside for recess?

15. Until we know that it is safe we shouldn't travel there.

Whose Cookie?

Add an **apostrophe** and an **s** to most singular nouns to form a possessive. When the noun ends with an **s** or **z** sound, add an apostrophe to form the possessive. When a singular noun is just one syllable, add an **apostrophe** and an **s**.

Examples: My brother's glove, Dennis' house, Gus's baseball

There is one chocolate chip cookie left, and it belongs to someone in the class. Fill in the missing apostrophes in the sentences below. Use the clues to decide whose cookie it is, and write the name on the line.

1. Lucas cookie is sitting on his desk.

2. Lucas sister cookie is in her mouth.

3. One cookie is in William pocket.

4. Another cookie is in Ross drawer.

5. Mrs. Phillips saw Casey cookie on his chair.

6. Brad said that he would grab a cookie after Rufus cookie was eaten.

7. Rufus said that he would wait until Melissa sister had eaten her cookie.

8. Melissa sister was waiting for Lucas mother to bring some milk.

9. Lucas mother is now running up the stairs to Mrs. Phillips classroom.

10. Lucas mother legs are short; so one person will have to wait for a cookie.

    The cookie belongs to _____.

Daily Skill-Builders Grammar & Usage 5–6
walch.com © 2004 Walch Publishing

Make It Theirs

For plural nouns ending in **s**, just add an **apostrophe** to make the nouns possessive. For plural nouns that don't end in **s**, add an **apostrophe** and an **s**. When more than one person shares the same possession, add an **s** to the last name. When two or more persons possess something as individuals, each name has an apostrophe.

Examples: We went to the **girls'** game on Saturday.

He took the **team's** picture.

Tim, John, and Bill's parents came to the game.

Jill's, Jim's, and John's lunches were all lost.

Make the following plural nouns possessive. Write them on the lines.

1. The children museum opens on Friday. _____

2. Those boys desks are very dirty. _____

3. The women locker is down the hall on the right. _____

4. Ryan, Catherine, and Isabel presents will be here tomorrow. _____

5. I wish that I had seen Erin and Sara presentation. _____

6. All of the teachers children are coming to the picnic. _____

7. The cats paws look like they were dunked in mud. _____

8. That should be the entire class decision. _____

9. All of the chickens eggs are orange. _____

10. The band concert will be on Wednesday. _____

11. Sharon watches are on the couch. _____

12. The nurses patients will be moved to a different wing. _____

The Amazing Apostrophe

Use an **apostrophe** to form the plural of a letter or number. Use an **apostrophe** to show that numbers or letters have been left out.

Examples: B's, 9's, class of '06, put the puddin' on the plate

Fill in the missing apostrophes in the sentences below.

1. George got As and Bs on his report card.

2. I am in the class of 05, and my brother is in the class of 08.

3. We want to take a vacation in 07.

4. My mom can't tell the 8s from the 3s without her glasses.

5. I was yellin cause it was really painful.

6. My aunt was born during the blizzard of 88.

7. All of the 5s and 2s are missing from the deck of cards.

8. Someone crossed out all of the Os on the sign.

9. I got a big bump, but I'm stayin in the game.

10. We all remember the hurricane of 94.

Daily Skill-Builders Grammar & Usage 5–6
walch.com © 2004 Walch Publishing

Contraction Action

Use an **apostrophe** to show that one or more letters are missing in a contraction.

Write the contraction for each pair of words on the line.

1. could not _____

2. will not _____

3. did not _____

4. I did _____

5. I will _____

6. they would _____

7. do not _____

8. they will _____

9. would not _____

10. they are _____

Read each contraction. Write the words the contraction stands for on the line.

11. isn't _____

12. it's _____

13. I've _____

14. she's _____

15. doesn't _____

16. shan't _____

17. hasn't _____

18. haven't _____

19. you'd _____

20. she'll _____

Say What?

Use **quotation marks** to show exactly what a speaker said. Put periods and commas *inside* quotation marks.

Example: "We will go on a field trip tomorrow," said the teacher.

When a question mark or an exclamation point punctuates the quotation, place it *inside* the quotation marks. If it punctuates the main sentence, put the question or exclamation mark *outside* the quotation marks.

Examples: "Should we bring them peaches?" asked Tania.
Did you hear Georgia say, "They already have some peaches"?

You are a reporter assigned to cover a road race. Fill in the missing quotation and punctuation marks in the sentences below.

1. The mayor said This will be the best and biggest race in the town's history

2. One leading contender asked Will there be a large crowd

3. There will be at least half of the town at the race the mayor said.

4. Did anyone hear the organizers say We expect to see a thousand people there

5. The race will start at Ocean Drive and end at Hill Crest Road said the race's director.

6. I am confident that I will win said Garrett Billings from Oklahoma.

7. Do you know how difficult it is to train for this asked racer Gail Bradley.

8. Will there be people around to help a racer if he or she says I need water

9. I bring my entire family to see the race says Ryan Vandorse.

10. Whoever wins this race will have a good shot at the Olympics said the race's director.

Daily Skill-Builders Grammar & Usage 5–6
walch.com © 2004 Walch Publishing

Carry on the Conversation

Imagine that two friends are having an argument about who is the better baseball player. Write ten more sentences continuing the conversation.

"I scored two runs in the last game," said Manny.

"Yes, but who drove you in?" asked Nate.

1. _____

2. _____

3. _____

4. _____

5. _____

6. _____

7. _____

8. _____

9. _____

10. _____

Popping Parentheses

Use **parentheses** around words that make an idea clearer or that adds information.

Examples: We provided the entertainment **(playing the drums)** for the parents. **(makes an idea clearer)**

You should take the shortcut **(Shelley Street)** to get there. **(adds information)**

The following words in parentheses have popped out of the sentences. Mark where the words should be added to the sentences. The first one has been done for you.

(figure 7)
1. Turn to the figure to see the chart on speed limits.

(clapping loudly)
2. We showed our approval of the musician's performance.

(Wildrose Street)
3. I live on a quiet side street on the west side of town.

(the gray one)
4. I left my coat at Joanne's house.

(using a bird call)
5. The girl called the sparrow to her.

(running quickly)
6. We made it home before the rain started.

(Montreal)
7. I am going to my favorite city next week.

(Mr. Neale)
8. We saw our neighbor working around his bushes.

(A's and B's)
9. I received good grades on my report card.

(laughing loudly)
10. We made a disturbance in the hallway.

Daily Skill-Builders Grammar & Usage 5–6
walch.com © 2004 Walch Publishing

Capture the Colons

Use a **colon** to introduce a list that comes after a complete sentence. Do not use a colon after a verb or a preposition.

Examples: We brought many things for lunch: sandwiches, chips, soda, and cookies.

My bed is made of cherry, oak, and maple wood.

Draw a circle around the colons in the sentences below that don't belong there.

1. We made a card using: construction paper, glue, and glitter.

2. I bought three things at the garage sale: a bike, a book, and a lamp.

3. We saw three of my aunts there: Aunt Jennifer, Aunt Sonia, and Aunt Tania.

4. My favorite songs include: "Way to Go," "Happy Days," and "Blue Skies."

5. Firefighters need the following items: hoses, ladders, and axes.

6. We should make a salad of: anchovies, green peppers, and black olives.

7. My best friends are coming: Yoshi, Beth, and Sue.

8. I brought my favorite sundae toppings: chocolate sauce, strawberries, and nuts.

9. We saw some large animals at the zoo: giraffes, bears, and buffalo.

10. We left the fair with: balloon animals, stuffed animals, and cherry pie.

Shopping List

Use a **colon** to introduce a list that comes after a complete sentence. Don't use a colon after a verb or a preposition.

Examples: I love three types of flowers: roses, sunflowers, and peonies.

My father's favorite foods include spaghetti, enchiladas, and egg rolls.

Write a sentence for each group of items listed below. Use a colon to introduce each list.

1. ski poles   skis   sunglasses

   _____

2. rabbits   chipmunks   squirrels

   _____

3. chocolate   vanilla   strawberry

   _____

4. a hammer   nails   a screwdriver

   _____

5. jelly beans   licorice   bubblegum

   _____

6. rubies   emeralds   diamonds

   _____

7. a camera   film   a case

   _____

8. a doctor   a dentist   a ballerina

   _____

9. a brush   a canvas   paint

   _____

10. a pitchfork   hay   seeds

    _____

Daily Skill-Builders Grammar & Usage 5–6
walch.com © 2004 Walch Publishing

Slip in a Semicolon

Use a **semicolon** to join two independent clauses if there isn't a coordinating conjunction between them.

> **Example:** My dad loves to watch me swim; he goes to all of my swim meets.

Fill in the missing semicolons in the sentences below.

1. My dentist likes crocodiles there are pictures of crocodiles hanging on his ceiling.

2. A couple of snowflakes landed on my tongue catching snowflakes is a lot of fun.

3. We arrived at the dance late I want to be early next time.

4. My cousin bought a new skateboard I wish I were old enough to have one.

5. The kangaroo jumped over the fence kangaroos can jump very, very high.

6. I saw a seal in the harbor this morning however, I only saw it for a second.

7. The water in the pitcher is too cold my teeth are very sensitive.

8. We saw a flock of birds fly over us they must be flying south for the winter.

9. I want to ride the yellow bumper cars I wish that I had brought more money.

10. I gave Alysha the yellow one maybe I will get a blue one the next time.

Semicolons Go Marching

Use a **semicolon** when items in a series are long and complex. Semicolons help to clarify the separate items and meanings.

> **Example:** We ate lunch at the diner; went shopping for shoes, hats, and gloves; and then had dinner at a restaurant.

Fill in the missing semicolons in the sentences below.

1. We took a boat ride roasted vegetables, hot dogs, and marshmallows and lay in the sun.

2. The mechanic tested the brakes, the steering wheel, and the horn fixed the engine and replaced the headlight.

3. We could skate on the pond, in the arena, or on the lake go sledding or build a snow fort.

4. Michael and Megan packed sunscreen, bathing suits, and towels drove to the beach and swam with Tim, Sheri, and Kyle.

5. I like to play dominoes, checkers, and chess read books and watch television.

6. My cat likes to play with yarn, balls, and cat toys scratch the sofa and sleep on my feet.

7. We drove five hours to the campsite unpacked our tents, sleeping bags, and clothing and finally went to bed.

8. The coach blew the whistle pointed at Kim, Kayla, and Karen and then took them out of the game.

9. My parents drove us to camp waved good-bye to my brother, my sister, and me and then they drove away.

10. The author read from her latest book signed some autographs for Sharif, Jason, and Keri and then went home to start writing another book.

Hy·phen·ate

Use a **hyphen** to divide a word at the end of a page. Always put the hyphen between two syllables. Never divide a one-syllable word. Never put a hyphen after a one-letter syllable. Never divide contractions.

Examples: Environment can be divided in three places: *en-vi-ron-ment*.
Don't do the following: gre-at, i-dentity, have-n't.

Circle the words below that can be hyphenated. For these words, put hyphens where you can divide the word, and write the word on the line. The first one has been done for you.

1. camera

   cam-er-a

2. meal

   _____

3. warehouse

   _____

4. can't

   _____

5. failure

   _____

6. impeach

   _____

7. gale

   _____

8. event

   _____

9. region

   _____

10. ivory

    _____

11. ark

    _____

12. pilgrim

    _____

13. perk

    _____

14. utopia

    _____

15. gust

    _____

16. increase

    _____

Word-Maker!

Use a **hyphen** to join two words that can form an adjective before a noun. Use a hyphen to form new words that begin with **self, ex, great, all,** and **half.**

Examples: **Blue-green** sea, **brother-proof** desk **(adjectives before a noun)**
Self-made, great-uncle **(new words)**

Use the words and prefixes in the box to form some new words. Write as many words as you can think of on the lines. Write a noun after the adjectives you form.

ex	made	self	proof	spider
half	brand	sister	grandfather	new
great	washed	blue	white	purpose
grin	big	all	boss	faded

_____ _____ _____

_____ _____ _____

_____ _____ _____

_____ _____ _____

_____ _____ _____

_____ _____ _____

_____ _____ _____

_____ _____ _____

_____ _____ _____

Daily Skill-Builders Grammar & Usage 5–6
walch.com © 2004 Walch Publishing

Helpful Hyphens

Use a **hyphen** in some compound words. Use a hyphen between the numbers in a fraction. Use a hyphen to join a letter to a word.

Examples: Well-done **(compound word)**, one-tenth **(fraction)**, x-ray **(join a letter)**

Fill in any missing hyphens in the sentences below.

1. My mom bought some fat free ice cream for dessert.

2. I have only cleaned one fourth of the windows.

3. Do you like your steak well done?

4. The police officer wears a bullet proof vest.

5. I have a t ball game at noon tomorrow.

6. One third of my well worn jeans is covered in mud.

7. The cookies were half baked, so they were a little soft.

8. My dog only ate one fourth of its meal.

9. I have already sent you an e mail about it.

10. We had a first class cruise to Aruba.

Use a **hyphen** to divide a word that appears at the end of a line. Draw a circle around the words below that could be hyphenated if they appeared at the end of a line. Fill in the hyphen(s).

11. ran   12. super   13. identity   14. diver

15. can't   16. ignore   17. environment   18. danger

A Sudden Dash!

Use a **dash** to show an obvious and sudden break in a sentence.

Example: The trip tomorrow—if you didn't already know—has been canceled.

Fill in the missing dashes in the sentences below.

1. We went to a park I may have already told you this to listen to a concert.

2. We brought along a picnic we always do so that we could stay there the whole day.

3. My three best friends came with me you know them along with my dog Ralph.

4. There was a large crowd there always is to see the band.

5. The band plays a mix of music in case you didn't know that appeals to many people.

6. We put our blanket near the pond we like the water and sat down.

7. We had a large blue blanket you know which one that everyone could sit on.

8. There were birds in the pond nearby as there always are that made some noise.

9. The concert started late I was a little annoyed but everyone was happy to hear the music.

10. Suddenly, my cat Ralph took off you know how that cat likes to run into the field to chase the mice!

Daily Skill-Builders Grammar & Usage 5–6
walch.com © 2004 Walch Publishing

We Interrupt This Program...

Use a **dash** to emphasize a word, a series of words, or a phrase. Also, use a dash to show that another person is interrupting someone's speech.

Examples: You will find many books—history books, fiction books, guides—at the library.

Hello, well—yes, I would love to—yes, that's a good time—yes, good, I will pick you up.

Fill in the missing dashes that emphasize certain words, series, and phrases.

1. I broke three parts of my body my arm, my leg, and my ankle when I fell off the roof.

2. We only go to my grandmother's house for one holiday Christmas during the school year.

3. I have many hobbies building toys, racing cars, and playing baseball that I enjoy.

4. You can buy many things paper towels, vegetables, and hammers at the general store.

5. I want to visit many cities Paris, London, Hong Kong during my lifetime.

Joanna and Jenny are having a conversation. Write a dash whenever someone is interrupted.

6. **Joanna:** Hi, Jenny, how are

7. **Jenny:** I am so glad you called Joanna! I have so much to tell you!

8. **Joanna:** Oh, good, I can't wait to hear.

9. **Jenny:** Did you

10. **Joanna:** Wait! Is this about Mrs. Crenshaw?

11. **Jenny:** Of course it

12. **Joanna:** Because I don't want to

13. **Jenny:** I know you don't want to know.

14. **Joanna:** That's right, so

15. **Jenny:** It's not about Mrs. Crenshaw, so let me tell the story!

A Barrel of Brackets

Use **brackets** to set off words that explain something in quoted language or within parentheses. Also, use brackets when you have to add or change a word in a quotation.

Examples: The race-car driver said that he would "win the next race **[the Indianapolis 500]** this year."

The mayor told me he "will do all that **[he]** can to win the race."

Fill in the missing brackets in the sentences below.

1. A doctor is quoted as saying that "one hospital has too many beds, while the other Waldorf County Hospital has too few."

2. Mrs. Stimpson, a local elementary school teacher, said, "My school Lyndon Elementary needs renovations."

3. Mr. Blackwell, the fire chief, is quoted as saying "Mr. Shirwell, the new fireman at Firehouse 80 will be a good fit."

4. Mr. Cox, the principal, told an assembly of teachers this morning that "Mrs. Bonny the retiring teacher at Sherwood Elementary will be sorely missed."

5. The governor told the Clarksville City Council on Tuesday that he wouldn't "drop funding for either Morrisville or his town Clarksville."

The sentences that follow have quoted material that needs to change to fit the sentence. Use bracketed words to change each quotation. The first one has been done for you.

6. My band teacher told us that he "~~don't~~ [doesn't] want to hear ~~you~~ [us] play that song ever again!"

7. The clown said that he "always try to make people laugh if I can."

8. The artist said that she "paint landscapes more often than people."

9. The construction worker explained that the work "will continue until my men are finished."

10. We have a long drive, so the bus driver said that we could eat "as long as I don't have to clean anything up."

Daily Skill-Builders Grammar & Usage 5–6
walch.com © 2004 Walch Publishing

Finishing Touches

Fill in the missing **end marks** and **commas** in the sentences below.

1. Did you hear the news about the world's largest slide

2. My little sister was born on May 10 1997 in Tulsa Oklahoma

3. Be careful of the long jagged stick in the road

4. Wow this is going to be fantastic

5. Yes I think that completing a marathon is a wonderful goal

6. Jane would you bring these plates to Uncle Harry

7. We moved to Portland Oregon in late December

8. If you want to see the space shuttle lift-off you should go to Florida

9. Ouch that crab's claws really hurt

10. We ate dinner washed the dishes and went to bed

11. Rebecca the sticky slimy gooey mess must be cleaned up now

12. My Aunt Robin a wonderful artist painted all of our portraits

13. When you are at camp would you write to me

14. Oh no that is terrible shocking news

15. I picked some berries and then I made a mud pie

Missing Marks

Fill in the missing **apostrophes** (and *s*'s if needed) and **quotation marks** in the sentences below.

1. I ate all of Cheryl ice cream when she wasn't looking.

2. Dad said, Dont leave without saying good-bye.

3. Did you hear Tim say, This house is haunted?

4. The boys team practices in the afternoon.

5. The children toys are in the playroom downstairs.

6. I cant borrow Casey skateboard because its broken.

7. Dont use all of the pepper, Dad said.

8. Gus house is down the street from a cemetery.

9. We should bring the Smith dog inside the house.

10. The rabbit fur is a beautiful shade of gray.

11. I took Mark and David place in line.

12. Why cant you bring Ralph surfboard to the beach? said Nancy.

13. You shouldnt sleep in the tent tonight, said Jackie.

14. The band instruments are still on the bus.

15. We couldnt bring all of the girls shoes.

Daily Skill-Builders Grammar & Usage 5–6
walch.com © 2004 Walch Publishing

Punctuation Panic!

Fill in the missing **colons** and **semicolons**.

1. I want a few things from the store lettuce, ketchup, and blueberries.

2. My aunt loves to go waterskiing she should buy a boat.

3. I took the test on Friday I hope I passed.

4. Please bring the following items duct tape, a screwdriver, and a saw.

5. My mom always uses the same ingredients butter, flour, and eggs.

Fill in the missing **hyphens**, **dashes**, and **brackets**.

6. The winner said that "he trained long and hard for the race."

7. One of the wheels on your bike if you didn't notice is flat.

8. We watched the waves break on a blue green sea.

9. My dream you may already know this is to be a jet pilot.

10. The clown said that "he liked to make people laugh, so he joined the circus."

11. My great aunt is staying at our house next week.

12. We ate one fourth of the pie and saved the rest for later.

13. I have a T-shirt you may have seen it that says "Smile."

14. The singer was a little off key this afternoon.

15. The little dog you know which one I mean ran away this morning.

Spotlight the Subjects

A **subject** is the word in the sentence that does something. A subject could also be the word that is talked about.

Examples: **Tracy** hopped over the hole.
He was a talented pianist.

Draw a circle around the subjects in the following sentences.

1. Carrie swam in the lake at the park on Saturday.

2. Brad always builds forts out of big pieces of wood.

3. Yes, they were always nice to me.

4. Mrs. Ratchet will bring her famous squash casserole to the dinner.

5. Mark spies on his little brother and his friends.

6. Wendy shook the president's hand after his speech.

7. She is the best tennis player in the state.

8. He was the best student in Mrs. Jacob's class.

9. Marty plays basketball every day after school.

10. Rabbits can move very quickly when they're scared.

11. The ball rolled down the hill and into the street.

12. We are the best team in the league.

13. The watch died when it fell in the water.

14. Maybe Sergio is playing golf right now.

15. The apples fall to the ground when there's a strong wind.

Daily Skill-Builders Grammar & Usage 5–6
walch.com © 2004 Walch Publishing

Something to Talk About

A **subject** is the word in the sentence that does something or is talked about.

> **Examples:** **Jordan** races toy cars.
>
> Yes, **she** is a very nice person.

Underline the subjects in the sentences below.

Our Museum Trip

Yesterday, we went to the city. We went to see an exhibit at the museum. The exhibit was on the Mayan ruins. Our family read about it in the paper. We thought that it looked interesting.

We had to drive for a long time to get to the city. My brother got carsick twice. My sister played games. My mother helped me find license plates from different states. Everyone just wanted to get to the city.

The search for a parking space in the city took a long time. Mom found a sign for a parking garage, and we left it there. I was in charge of remembering the location.

The museum was very far from the parking garage. We had to walk a long way. My feet hurt from walking. After an hour, my family finally reached the museum. The steps up to the museum were steep and tiring. We were all exhausted.

Something looked odd in the museum. The police were inside looking around. We didn't see too many tourists. My father asked what happened. Oh no! Several artifacts on exhibit had been stolen! We never got to see the exhibit. The authorities are still looking for the culprit and the artifacts.

Savvy Subjects

A **subject** is the word in the sentence that does something or is talked about.

Examples: My best friend's brother **Juan** walks to school every morning.
My neighbor **Danielle** rides her bike to school.

Underline the subjects in the sentences below.

1. Perhaps our teacher Mrs. Jenkins will sing for us at the concert.

2. Yesterday my best friend came into our store.

3. I would love to ride on your new bicycle!

4. The newest house on the block is falling apart!

5. Perhaps the ballpoint pens would work better.

6. The sticky mess smells awful!

7. We heard some very beautiful music.

8. Susan's mother's friend is coming, too.

9. Our old grill is practically falling over.

10. A brand new convertible just drove by.

11. The baby fish are tickling my toes.

12. My best friend, Jack, gave Kara a flower.

13. My dad's computer is broken.

14. My mom's cousins always bring seafood to the family reunion.

15. The little gray mouse scampered across the floor.

Daily Skill-Builders Grammar & Usage 5–6
walch.com © 2004 Walch Publishing

A Peppering of Predicates

A **predicate (verb)** is the part of a sentence that tells what the **subject** is doing.

Examples: Sydney **sang** all of her favorite songs to the audience.
Our new puppy always **jumps** on my lap.

Underline the predicates in the story below.

A Delicious Dinner

I watch the cooks at the restaurant. Dana chops the vegetables into small pieces. Then he puts them into the frying pan. He turns the heat to high. He cooks the vegetables. The vegetables look scrumptious!

Rick peels potatoes with his potato peeler. He cuts them into chunks. He sprinkles salt and pepper on them. Then he roasts them in a pan in the oven. He places them on the top rack by the burner. The potatoes turn brown and crisp. They taste delicious!

Alice prepares the fish. She removes all of the scales from the fish. She chops off the head with her knife. Then she slices the fish down the middle. She takes out all of the bones. Then she cooks it in a pan. She flips the fish occasionally. She watches it carefully. She squeezes a little lemon juice on the fish. The fish smells yummy! The diners enjoy their dinner. They agree. The dinner tastes delicious.

Precious Predicates

A **predicate (verb)** is the part of a sentence that tells what the **subject** is doing.

   Example: We **washed** the carrots in cold water.

Underline the predicates in the sentences below.

1. A gopher dug a hole in the backyard.

2. Everyone rides the merry-go-round at the fair.

3. We melted butter for the popcorn.

4. Sheila painted a picture of a lighthouse.

5. We skipped stones on Joe's Pond.

6. I often whistle on the way to school.

7. We whispered the answer to Jackie.

8. I climbed to the top of the highest tree!

9. Ben crossed the finish line first.

10. I wished him a happy birthday yesterday.

11. The tomatoes turned red in the sunlight.

12. The papers slipped off the shelf onto the floor.

13. My favorite shoes squeak on wood floors.

14. The roses in the backyard smell divine.

15. Tim bakes apples with cinnamon and sugar.

Choose a Predicate

A **predicate (verb)** is the part of a sentence that tells what the **subject** is doing.

>   **Example:** The little tree **bends** in the breeze.

Complete each sentence below by writing a predicate on the line.

1. Tyson _____ the race through his binoculars.

2. I usually _____ at least five dollars to charity every month.

3. The magician _____ a white dove behind the blanket.

4. I _____ when I saw the elephants perform in the circus.

5. The teacher _____ us to do all of the exercises.

6. The small porch roof _____ us from the hail.

7. Kayla _____ her baseball card for mine.

8. The angry customer _____ that he get his money back.

9. My mom _____ her ankle when she fell on the dock.

10. The neighbor's cat _____ on the cricket outside.

Subjects Versus Predicates

A **subject** is the word in the sentence that does something or is talked about.
A **predicate (verb)** is the part of a sentence that tells what the **subject** is doing.

Draw a circle around each subject. Underline each predicate.

1. The girls down the hall laugh very loudly.

2. My sister's stuffed animal falls on the floor all the time.

3. We rode the elevator with a famous athlete.

4. The shorthaired monkeys make a lot of noise.

5. My friend's uncle coughs every day during the winter.

Write sentences using the words below. Make each noun a subject and make each verb a predicate.

6. queen   offered

   _____

7. caterpillar   crawled

   _____

8. Mr. Snider   consumed

   _____

9. detective   investigated

   _____

10. foot   crushed

   _____

Daily Skill-Builders Grammar & Usage 5–6
walch.com © 2004 Walch Publishing

Subject and Predicate Hunt

A **subject** is the word in the sentence that does something or is talked about.
A **predicate (verb)** is the part of a sentence that tells what the **subject** is doing.

Join the hunt. Find the subjects and predicates in the sentences below. Underline the subjects and circle the predicates.

1. The large humpback whale blew water into the air.

2. The tiny bracelet pinched my wrist.

3. Ted's father's glasses are on the edge of his desk.

4. We rolled the ball to the edge of the playground.

5. My mother's camera broke from being dropped.

6. The new students participated in the discussion.

7. A very good decorator converted our living room into an office.

8. My little boat drifted slowly down the river.

9. The scratchy wool irritated my skin.

10. My little plant sprouted a new branch.

11. The trombone players made lots of noise.

12. My family hummed the song in the car.

13. The new engineer surveyed the site.

14. The defendant in the case jumped out of his chair.

15. Volleyball players frequently dive onto the sand to get the ball.

Is It Natural?

A **natural subject** comes *before* the verb. An **inverted subject** comes *after* the verb.

Examples: Dorothy **was** here a second ago. **(natural subject)**
There **was** a **woman** here a second ago. **(inverted subject)**

Underline the subjects and predicates below. Write an **N** next to the sentences below that contain natural subjects. Write an **I** next to the sentences with inverted subjects.

____ 1. My chubby cat slides down the steps.

____ 2. "Listen to me!" cried the tour guide.

____ 3. Seldom have we seen so many swans in one place.

____ 4. Perhaps she pulled the string too tight.

____ 5. The cute, little dog howled at the moon.

____ 6. Past the gates and into the sunset rode the valiant knight.

____ 7. Even more important is the paragraph that gives your conclusion.

____ 8. Have you seen a red and white striped sweatshirt?

____ 9. The kitten licked all of the milk in its bowl.

____ 10. There was a ketchup bottle here this morning.

The Natural Way

A **natural subject** comes *before* the verb. An **inverted subject** comes *after* the verb.

Examples: My little **brother slid** down the banister onto the floor. **(natural subject)**
There **are** three **rabbits** in the cage. **(inverted subject)**

All of the sentences below have inverted subjects. Change the sentences to include natural subjects.

1. "I need some iced tea!" cried my mom.

   _____

2. Has Sandra heard the latest news about the mayor?

   _____

3. There were five jelly beans on the table.

   _____

4. Even more important is the word *can*.

   _____

5. "I am going insane!" whispered Mrs. Jacobs.

   _____

6. Over the hill and through the woods rode the lonely horseman.

   _____

7. There lies the grave of my great-great-grandfather.

   _____

8. Into the window flew the bat.

   _____

9. Even more noticeable is the stain on your dress.

   _____

10. Here stands the statue of the greatest woman alive.

   _____

What's the Difference?

A **natural subject** comes *before* the verb. An **inverted subject** comes *after* the verb.

Examples: **We rode** the ponies at the fair. **(natural subject)**
There **lies** the **home** of my ancestors. **(inverted subject)**

Write **N** next to the sentences that contain natural subjects. Write **I** next to the sentences that contain inverted subjects.

____ 1. The daisies fell over onto the ground.

____ 2. My largest bag ripped with the heavy groceries.

____ 3. Can Susie hear the loons calling?

____ 4. The neighbors sit on their lawn chairs in the summer.

____ 5. There hangs my favorite painting in the world.

____ 6. "Look out below!" cried the construction worker.

____ 7. Even funnier are the clowns in their costumes.

____ 8. The boat violently rocked back and forth.

____ 9. My little brother chases our pets around.

____ 10. There are too many chairs in this room.

Write sentences using the subjects and verbs listed below.

11. the storm   blew

    Natural subject: _____

12. Mrs. Smith   cooked

    Inverted subject: _____

13. My brothers   raced

    Natural subject: _____

14. The players   hit

    Natural subject: _____

15. The seagulls   are

    Inverted subject: _____

Be Agreeable!

Subjects and **predicates** must agree. Use a singular subject with a singular verb. Use a plural subject with a plural verb.

Examples: The **girls** next door **like** to swim in the pond.

Sammy's **dog chases** our cat.

solve	race	shrinks	suggest	paint
competes	eat	plays	insist	smells

Choose a verb from the box above, and write it on the line to complete each sentence.

1. Some artists on the beach _____ watercolors.

2. My little pink shirt _____ when you wash it, so be careful.

3. The team _____ very well this season.

4. The monkeys _____ bananas in their cages.

5. Milo and Alex _____ their boats on the stream.

6. We simply _____ that you take the trip.

7. The bouquet of flowers _____ so fragrant.

8. The students always _____ the math problems in an hour.

9. Leila _____ in the track meet tomorrow.

10. My cousins _____ that we visit this museum.

139

Let's Go to the Movies!

Subjects and **predicates** must agree. Use a singular subject with a singular verb. Use a plural subject with a plural verb.

Examples: Those **pens leak** all over my shirt.
The nice **boy** down the street **delivers** our paper.

Write the correct form of the verb on the lines below.

1. _____ (to be) you going to the movies with Sandra?

2. Sandra _____ (to want) to see the newest spy movie.

3. Bill and I _____ (to dislike) spy movies.

4. My family _____ (to see) a spy movie every week.

5. There _____ (to be) a better movie at the other theater.

6. "There'd better be a better movie!" _____ (to cry) Bill and Marty.

7. Through the rain and past the clouds _____ (to shine) a brilliant idea.

8. We will _____ (go) to this theater tonight and to the other theater tomorrow.

9. Bill _____ (to watch) movies all the time, so he won't mind seeing two.

10. I don't think there's a better solution, nor _____ (to do) Sandra.

Check It Out!

Subjects and **predicates** must agree. Use a singular subject with a singular verb. Use a plural subject with a plural verb.

Examples: Here **lies** the **beginning** of the highway to Florida.
The **butterflies** gently **float** on the summer breeze.

Put a check mark (✔) next to the sentences that agree.

____ **1.** The clocks chime every hour on the dot.

____ **2.** Is we going to the amusement park today?

____ **3.** The mice in the kitchen startle my mother.

____ **4.** Susie depend on the mailman to bring her the mail.

____ **5.** My sisters hesitates to tell me too much information.

____ **6.** I believe the man; so does my father.

____ **7.** With a bow enter the famous Mr. Sterling.

____ **8.** The sad music expresses powerful emotions.

____ **9.** The little kids always interrupts their parents.

____ **10.** "Help me lift this box!" cry Mr. Budge.

____ **11.** The plastic preserves the freshness of the crackers.

____ **12.** Has you seen the newest video game?

____ **13.** Peter and Nancy direct all of the school plays.

____ **14.** The papers fly all over the place when the window is open.

____ **15.** The flock of seagulls sits near the edge of the water.

The Show Must Go On!

Write an **S** over the subjects in the sentences below. Write a **P** over the predicates.

1. Kiley makes posters for our plays.

2. There is a play in this theater next week.

3. The actors don't have their costumes yet.

4. The director wants three more rehearsals.

5. The lights shine directly onto the stage.

6. Many parents volunteer backstage for the play.

7. The star actors come from the surrounding towns.

8. From the foothills, from the mountains, come the roaring crowds.

9. "Many people will come to the production," says the director.

10. Everyone hopes that the audience will enjoy it.

11. A camera films the play for a class.

12. A large number of seats are in the theater.

13. The band plays in front of the stage.

14. The audience surrounds the band.

15. Theater people work very, very hard.

Daily Skill-Builders Grammar & Usage 5–6
walch.com © 2004 Walch Publishing

Pop Quiz!

In the sentences below, write an **S** over the subjects. Write a **P** over the predicates.

1. The seal dove into the water in front of us.

2. The coins sink to the bottom of the well.

3. The acorns fell into our yard.

4. Maybe we saw a bald eagle.

5. Cynthia likes the sound of crickets at night.

Write **N** next to the sentences with natural subjects. Write **I** next to the sentences with inverted subjects. Cross out any verbs that don't agree, and write the correct form above the sentence.

___ 6. The horse trembles in the cold morning air.

___ 7. Even more important is the paper due next month.

___ 8. Have you seen this morning's paper?

___ 9. We welcomes all of the new neighbors.

___ 10. Here sit the great conductor, Mr. Schavone.

___ 11. I often refers to the dictionary for help with spelling.

___ 12. "You shouldn't neglect your responsibilities," says my father.

___ 13. I heartily accept the challenge.

___ 14. Into the dark of night flies the brave pilot.

___ 15. Seldom do the mother hen leave her nest.

Park Plans

Declarative sentences make statements. They give information about a person, a place, a thing, or an idea. They always end with a period.

> **Examples:** Tommy's bumper car bumped into mine.
>
> Trees provide important shade in the summer.

The mayor has just opened a new park in town. Circle the numer of each declarative sentence below and fill in the missing periods.

1. This park will be called Penelope Park

2. It will be named after a retired teacher, Penelope Parker

3. People may have a picnic here

4. Look out below

5. Next year we will build a bandstand

6. There will be free concerts here in the summer

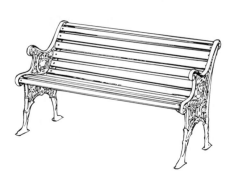

7. Will anyone attend the concerts

8. There will also be a pond in the center of the park

9. There will be ducks on the pond in the summer

10. There will be an ice-skating rink in the winter

11. We will plant two flower gardens

12. Does anyone know a good gardener

13. There will be paths through the gardens

14. Many people will visit the park on the weekends

15. Are there any questions

Curious Clara

Interrogative sentences ask questions. They are followed by a question mark.

    Example: Would you like to see my pet spider?

Clara is curious about everything. Write two interrogative sentences that Clara might ask about the information in each declarative sentence below.

We are going to Chicago this weekend.

1. _____

2. _____

I saw a whale in the harbor yesterday.

3. _____

4. _____

There will be a blizzard this weekend.

5. _____

6. _____

Our neighbor collects his own honey.

7. _____

8. _____

An astronaut came to our school today.

9. _____

10. _____

Beach Rules

An **imperative sentence** gives a command. It is always followed by a period.

Examples: Bring me some paper.

You must always watch where you are going.

A father is talking to his children about going to the beach. Circle the number of each imperative sentence below and fill in the missing periods.

1. Never swim by yourself

2. You must always wear sunscreen

3. The water is probably cold

4. Don't lose the beach ball

5. Put all of your trash in the trash bins

6. Do you want to bring the rafts

7. Never throw sand on other people

8. You must always listen to the lifeguard

9. There are sandwiches in the cooler

10. Do you want a ham sandwich

11. Bring your sandals

12. The sand will be hot

13. Don't throw rocks at the seagulls

14. Look after your little brother

15. Be nice to others

Daily Skill-Builders Grammar & Usage 5–6
walch.com © 2004 Walch Publishing

Fun in the Sea!

An **exclamatory sentence** shows strong emotion or surprise. It is punctuated by an exclamation point.

Example: Watch out for the snake**!**

Write an exclamation point after the sentences below that could be exclamatory.

1. I just petted a dolphin _____

2. Look at the stingrays _____

3. The ocean is called the Pacific Ocean _____

4. This is so much fun _____

5. Watch out for sharks _____

6. A baby eel just swam past my foot _____

7. Bring me a towel _____

8. A fish swam into my hand _____

9. Do you want to use my mask _____

10. Wow, that school of fish is huge _____

11. Look, there's a whale _____

12. I can't believe how many fish swim here _____

13. Lend me your snorkeling equipment_____

14. This is the best vacation ever _____

15. Can we swim again tomorrow _____

Sentence Sleuth

Write **D** after the declarative sentences, **I** after the interrogative sentences, **M** after the imperative sentences, and **E** after the exclamatory sentences below. Fill in the correct punctuation marks.

> A **declarative sentence** makes a statement.
>
> An **interrogative sentence** asks a question.
>
> An **imperative sentence** gives a command.
>
> An **exclamatory sentence** shows strong emotion or surprise.

1. Did you know that Whitney finished ahead of Dennis _____

2. Quebec is to the east of Montreal _____

3. Did you see Alyssa and Shawn on the television _____

4. Pass the mushrooms and potatoes _____

5. Oh no, there are spiders in the bathtub _____

6. Mrs. Cartridge is driving us to practice _____

7. Look at the huge rainbow _____

8. Never go anywhere with strangers _____

9. I just won a million dollars _____

10. I received three pairs of socks for Christmas from Uncle Peyton _____

11. Can we go to Cho's house for dinner _____

12. Bring the binoculars with the red stripe _____

13. There's a bat in my room _____

14. Vegetarians don't eat meat _____

15. Are Ennis and Jane coming over today _____

I.D. the Sentences

Check if the sentence types that are listed are correct. Write **T** for true and **F** for false on the lines below. Fill in the correct punctuation in the answer boxes.

> A **declarative sentence** makes a statement.
>
> An **interrogative sentence** asks a question.
>
> An **imperative sentence** gives a command.
>
> An **exclamatory sentence** shows strong emotion or surprise.

____ 1. Can you speak Spanish ☐ **Interrogative sentence**

____ 2. Tell me which position I will play today ☐ **Declarative sentence**

____ 3. Watch out for the falling rocks ☐ **Imperative sentence**

____ 4. Give these brownies to your teacher at school ☐ **Imperative sentence**

____ 5. Do you want me to teach you how to play chess ☐ **Exclamatory sentence**

____ 6. There's a spider crawling up my leg ☐ **Declarative sentence**

____ 7. Would you please bring my favorite sweatshirt ☐ **Interrogative sentence**

____ 8. The Eiffel Tower is located in Paris, France ☐ **Declarative sentence**

____ 9. Use a pencil when you take the exam ☐ **Imperative sentence**

____ 10. It's so terrible that you lost your wallet ☐ **Interrogative sentence**

____ 11. Can I go with you to the movie ☐ **Imperative sentence**

____ 12. Never leave the house without your keys ☐ **Declarative sentence**

____ 13. There are five Great Lakes in the United States ☐ **Exclamatory sentence**

____ 14. Look out for the fly ball ☐ **Interrogative sentence**

____ 15. Bring this hammer to your uncle ☐ **Imperative sentence**

Is It Simple?

A **simple sentence** states only one complete thought. A **compound sentence** is made up of two or more simple sentences joined by either a comma and a coordinating conjunction or a semicolon.

Examples: Jacob and Dylan sang and danced in class. **(simple sentence)**

I have tried those, but I didn't like the flavor. **(compound sentence)**

Write an **S** next to the simple sentences below. Write a **C** next to the compound sentences.

_____ 1. Mark and David live across the street from me.

_____ 2. My hands and feet look white and feel numb.

_____ 3. Bill and Sarah walked to Morrisville, but they drove the rest of the way.

_____ 4. My brother and I bought our mother a gift.

_____ 5. I always sing on the way to school.

_____ 6. My uncle is going to London; I wish I could go with him.

_____ 7. We could leave it here, or we could bring it with us.

_____ 8. I play soccer and read books.

_____ 9. Donald's piano looks new and sounds great.

_____ 10. I will play baseball today, and you will join me.

Sentence Construction

A **simple sentence** states only one complete thought. A **compound sentence** is made up of two or more simple sentences joined by either a comma and a coordinating conjunction or a semicolon.

Examples: Gerry and Tim finished the project on Tuesday. **(simple sentence)**
My parents bought me a ticket; I wish that I could go. **(compound sentence)**

Join the simple sentences together. Write the compound sentences on the lines below.

1. Bob likes to go waterskiing. He can't go very often.

   _____

2. They don't have any more shampoo. I can't wash my hair without it.

   _____

3. I am leaving for camp tomorrow. My sister is coming with me.

   _____

4. We could fish at the lake. We could fish in the river.

   _____

5. I want to paint a picture. I don't have any more paint.

   _____

6. The dog chewed on my homework. It ate our dessert.

   _____

7. My uncle bought a plane. I wish I were old enough to fly it.

   _____

8. We could play in the backyard. We could play at the neighbor's house.

   _____

9. The flowers in their yard are turning brown. They're falling over.

   _____

10. My mom is taking me to the baseball game. She is going to buy me a hot dog.

   _____

Tie Them Together

A **simple sentence** states only one complete thought. A **compound sentence** is made up of two or more simple sentences joined by either a comma and a coordinating conjunction or a semicolon.

Examples: The eggs and turkey look fresh and delicious. **(simple sentence)**

I am bringing a sweater**,** and I think you should, too. **(compound sentence)**

Draw a line connecting a simple sentence on the left to either a coordinating conjunction or a semicolon. Draw another line connecting the middle column to a simple sentence on the right. Write the compound sentences on the lines below.

Valerie bought eight raffle tickets.	;	I wish I could ride them.
My rabbit hopped out of the cage.	but	We could make dinner.
Jason and Tim bought new bikes.	and	I don't have enough money.
We could eat candy.	but	I won the prize.
I want those baseball cards.	or	It ate all of our carrots.

1. _____

_____

2. _____

_____

3. _____

_____

4. _____

_____

5. _____

_____

Daily Skill-Builders Grammar & Usage 5–6
walch.com © 2004 Walch Publishing

Make It Complex

A **complex sentence** contains one independent clause and at least one dependent clause. A dependent clause begins with a subordinating conjunction (*after, although, because, when, since, unless, while,* and so forth) or a relative pronoun (*who, what, that,* and so forth).

> **Examples: Because** the field was wet, the game was canceled. **(subordinating conjunction)**
>
> The coach, **who** was not very happy, went home. **(relative pronoun)**

Make complex sentences out of the phrases and simple sentences below. If needed, use the following subordinating conjunctions: *when, while, after, because,* and *since.* The first one has been done for you.

1. We can't play outside. We should see a movie.
   <u>Since we can't play outside, we should see a movie.</u>

2. The gold and silver box contains a lot of money. which we found on the street
   _____

3. You may choose a sugar cereal for your birthday. whichever you want
   _____

4. We ran out of gas. Our car stopped running.
   _____

5. You finish your homework. You may go to the park.
   _____

6. He is finished making dinner. He will make dessert.
   _____

7. My sister has very good fashion sense. whose shirt I am wearing
   _____

8. I bought some ice cream at the grocery store. you told me to buy it
   _____

9. The band was practicing. I couldn't hear you talk.
   _____

10. The man in the corner is the cousin of my best friend's father. who was dancing
    _____

From Simple to Complex

A **complex sentence** contains one independent clause and at least one dependent clause. A dependent clause begins with a subordinating conjunction (*after, although, because, when,* and so forth) or a relative pronoun (*who, what, that,* and so forth).

Examples: The woman **who** coughs loudly, is my aunt. **(relative pronoun)**

After we packed, we moved into our new house. **(subordinating conjunction)**

Make each simple sentence below complex by adding a phrase from the box. Write the new sentences on the lines.

which we ate rapidly	who is sitting at the corner table
Before I had the pie	Since Karen can't come here
Because it's warm outside	whose camera I'm using
whatever you'd like	After I finish my chores
whichever you want	While you were sleeping

1. We can't go skiing.

_____

2. That girl is my brother's girlfriend.

_____

3. You may buy one game at the store.

_____

4. I can go outside to play.

_____

5. You snored very loudly.

_____

6. My father is a great photographer.

_____

7. I ate a turkey sandwich.

_____

8. Buy some soda at the grocery store.

_____

9. We bought ice cream at the fair.

_____

10. We should go to Karen's house.

_____

Complex Charades

A **complex sentence** contains one independent clause and at least one dependent clause. A dependent clause begins with a subordinating conjunction (*after, although, because, when,* and so forth) or a relative pronoun (*who, what, that,* and so forth).

> **Examples:** **Before** getting out of the pool, Amy swam another lap. **(subordinating conjunction)**
>
> I saw that man, **who** gave us the card, at the store. **(relative pronoun)**

Make the sentences below complex sentences by adding the letter that corresponds with one of the phrases in the box.

a. which I love to do	**b.** Since I've cut my hair
c. who sells cars	**d.** While I move like I'm swimming
e. whose career is a doctor	**f.** which look like antlers
g. When I feel your wrist	**h.** whichever is closest
i. Because cooks mix food	**j.** Although I can't make any noise

1. I put my fingers, _____, on the top of my head to show I'm a deer.

2. _____, I am trying to be a fish.

3. _____, I am checking for a pulse like a doctor does.

4. I jump up and down, _____, to show that I am gymnast.

5. I point to a book, _____, to show that I am a student.

6. I point to my father, _____, to show that I am a doctor.

7. _____, I try to laugh to show I'm a clown.

8. _____, I pretend that I'm stirring to show I'm a chef.

9. I point to my uncle, _____, to show I'm a salesman.

10. _____, I haven't been able to pretend that I'm Goldie Locks.

Sentence Type?

A **simple sentence** states only one complete thought. A **compound sentence** is made up of two or more simple sentences joined by either a comma and a coordinating conjunction or a semicolon.

A **complex sentence** contains one independent clause and at least one dependent clause. A dependent clause begins with a subordinating conjunction (*after, although, because,* and so forth) or a relative pronoun (*who, what, that,* and so forth).

Read and decide the type of each sentence below. Write **SS** for simple sentence, **CP** for compound sentence, and **CX** for complex sentence.

1. Jack and I ran all the way to school. _____

2. Megan and Marsha sliced and baked the apples. _____

3. Because I can't see very well, I sit toward the front of the class. _____

4. I love to listen to music, but I don't have a stereo. _____

5. My dog is sick; we're taking Spike to the veterinarian today. _____

6. Sue sees many things from her window. _____

7. Mr. Howard, who spoke to our class, used to be my neighbor. _____

8. I cut and sew my own clothing. _____

9. While you were gone, we built another room. _____

10. We could go there now, or we could wait until later. _____

So Many Sentences

A **simple sentence** states only one complete thought. A **compound sentence** is made up of two or more simple sentences joined by either a comma and a coordinating conjunction or a semicolon.

A **complex sentence** contains one independent clause and at least one dependent clause. A dependent clause begins with a subordinating conjunction (*after, although, because, while,* and so forth) or a relative pronoun (*who, what, that,* and so forth).

Read each sentence and decide what type it is. Write **SS** for simple sentence, **CP** for compound sentence, and **CX** for complex sentence.

1. I go away to summer camp every year. _____

2. Gus saw a snake in the backyard; I am not going back there. _____

3. I would love to come with you, but I have to baby-sit. _____

4. My shoes and socks are covered with mud. _____

5. While you were reading your book, three planes flew overhead. _____

6. My cat will come home, or he will sleep outside. _____

7. You may borrow a book, whichever you'd like, for the weekend. _____

8. My little sister ate all of the blueberries; I wish there were more. _____

9. I like to run and sing across the meadow. _____

10. Because the soup is very hot, I think you will need to wait to eat it. _____

Abracadabra!

A **simple sentence** states only one complete thought. A **compound sentence** is made up of two or more simple sentences joined by either a comma and a coordinating conjunction or a semicolon.

A **complex sentence** contains one independent clause and at least one dependent clause. A dependent clause begins with a subordinating conjunction (*after, although, because, while*, and so forth) or a relative pronoun (*who, what, that, which*, and so forth).

Turn each sentence below into the type of sentence listed by either adding or removing a phrase.

1. The rabbits escaped out of their cage.

   Complex sentence: _____

2. I want to go on the ride, but I'm not tall enough.

   Simple sentence: _____

3. We could bring along some apples.

   Compound sentence: _____

4. My sister got a new scooter; I want to ride it later.

   Simple sentence: _____

5. I blew out the candles on the cake.

   Complex sentence: _____

6. I love to go fishing.

   Compound sentence: _____

7. I saw the baby at the park with her mom.

   Complex sentence: _____

8. I am moving to New York City; you should come, too.

   Simple sentence: _____

9. I wrote two songs this morning.

   Complex sentence: _____

10. Kim has a camp on Cliff Island.

    Compound sentence: _____

Daily Skill-Builders Grammar & Usage 5–6
walch.com © 2004 Walch Publishing

They Can Stand Alone!

An **independent clause** can stand alone as a complete sentence. A **clause** is a group of words that contains a subject and a predicate.

Circle the number of the shapes below that contain independent clauses. Write a period at the end of each independent clause.

1. The rose smelled divine

2. Kathy's big red

3. My bike squeaks

4. The ball rolls quickly

5. Jim and I walk

6. Sue goes running

7. My head and arms

8. Wet, slippery, and slimy

9. The boy is very tall

10. Ran the other way

11. Yo-yos are fun

12. The birds are chirping

Be Independent!

An **independent clause** can stand alone as a sentence.

Example: The dog ran to the fence.

Make independent clauses out of the words below.

1. Green, slimy snakes _____

2. Super-squishy sponges _____

3. My best friend Rick _____

4. Summer vacation last year _____

5. Wake up _____

6. The deep-sea diver _____

7. Bring _____

8. Hamburgers and hot dogs _____

9. Look for _____

10. My sunglasses _____

I Depend on You

A **dependent clause** cannot stand alone as a sentence.

Example: if the rain stops

Dependent clauses need to latch onto more words to become a sentence. Circle the dependent clauses below.

1. when I go biking

2. stop chewing gum

3. as long as you go

4. I like the rain

5. while I was napping

6. because it's late

7. leave the flowers alone

8. please walk now

9. since it is snowing

10. though I don't know

11. as if it were difficult

12. before we play

Do You Depend on Me?

A **dependent clause** cannot stand alone as a sentence.

Example: because we want to

Read the clauses below. If a clause is dependent, add other words to make it independent, and write it on the line. If the clause is already independent, leave it as is.

1. before you order _____

2. don't run across the street _____

3. since we can't see _____

4. while the water is running _____

5. unless we can't go _____

6. wrap a towel around it _____

7. he likes potato soup _____

8. although I didn't hear it _____

9. because it is hot _____

10. after you finish that _____

11. so that it doesn't leak _____

12. we swim often _____

Daily Skill-Builders Grammar & Usage 5–6
walch.com © 2004 Walch Publishing

Independent or Dependent?

An **independent clause** can stand alone as a sentence. A **dependent clause** cannot stand alone as a sentence.

Examples: I laughed for a long time. **(independent clause)**
when it's high tide **(dependent clause)**

Write **I** next to the independent clauses below, capitalize the first word, and write a period after the sentence. Write **D** next to the dependent clauses.

_____ 1. unless you can make it disappear

_____ 2. ride the pony over there

_____ 3. since the line is so long

_____ 4. although you just arrived

_____ 5. Grace and Martha gave me the camera

_____ 6. Jordan laughs and sings all the time

_____ 7. whereas there are never any pencils here

_____ 8. she doesn't want to be bothered

_____ 9. so that you don't make a mess

_____ 10. we should slide down the slide

More and More Clauses

An **independent clause** can stand alone as a sentence. A **dependent clause** cannot stand alone as a sentence.

Examples: I caught four fish. **(independent clause)**
so you should come **(dependent clause)**

If the clauses are independent, capitalize and punctuate them. If they are dependent, leave them alone.

1. as if money fell from the sky

2. some coins are beautiful

3. as long as Sandra has directions

4. if there it is free

5. the potatoes are still cooking

6. don't run with a stick

7. when the moon is full

8. please bring a camera

9. Casey likes to dance

10. as though I were still on the boat

11. Mrs. Santiago will come soon

12. because the ferry ride is too long

A Picnic of Prepositions

A **prepositional phrase** includes a preposition and an object of the preposition. A prepositional phrase may also contain words that modify the object.

> **Example:** The moths ate a hole **in the wool blanket.**
> (*In* is the preposition, *blanket* is the object of the preposition, and *the* and *wool* modify *blanket*.)

Underline the prepositional phrases below. Draw a circle around the prepositions.

1. The ball rolled underneath Cheryl's bed.

2. We sat upon the flat rocks.

3. Throughout the evening, we could hear the crickets chirping.

4. You have to lean toward the left side.

5. Our shoes and clothes are inside the cabin.

6. There is a skunk below the deck.

7. I sat between my aunt and uncle.

8. The ball landed near the sidelines.

9. My cat jumped onto the counter.

10. Mom drove through the tunnels.

11. We have all seen the exhibit at the museum.

12. My Uncle Roger and Aunt Helen are from Sweden.

13. I wore earplugs during the concert.

14. There are many rooms aboard the USS *Cole*.

15. You have to keep the ball within the limits.

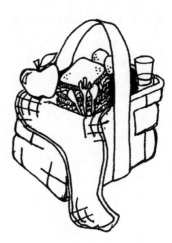

Play Ball!

A **prepositional phrase** includes a preposition and an object of the preposition. A prepositional phrase may also contain words that modify the object.

> **Example:** He already put the eggs **inside the paper bag.**
> (*Inside* is the preposition, *bag* is the object of the preposition, and *the* and *paper* modify *bag*.)

Circle the prepositional phrases in the sentences below.

1. A group of friends were playing pass on the playground.

2. Mike threw the ball to Cindy.

3. Cindy missed the ball, so it rolled toward the swings.

4. The ball went past the recess teacher.

5. The ball hit the pole and landed under the swing.

6. Terry retrieved the ball and threw it between Trevor and Nancy.

7. Trevor caught the ball with his glove.

8. He threw it across the playground.

9. Anna caught the ball near the fence.

10. She threw it to Mike, who threw it again to Cindy.

Daily Skill-Builders Grammar & Usage 5–6
walch.com © 2004 Walch Publishing

The Treasure Chest

A **prepositional phrase** includes a preposition and an object of the preposition. A prepositional phrase may also contain words that modify the object.

Example: We like to go to the park **near the flower shop.**
(*Near* is the preposition, *shop* is the object of the preposition, and *the* and *flower* modify *shop*.)

Underline the prepositions below. Circle the objects of the prepositions.

1. We found an old chest above my grandmother's garage.

2. The chest was hidden beneath an old blanket.

3. There was a beautiful gold key inside the lock.

4. We turned the key and lifted the top toward the ceiling.

5. A few moths and other bugs flew out the top.

6. We peered inside and first saw a letter stuck between two books.

7. There were many objects around the books.

8. There was clothing toward the back.

9. There were stacks of shoes toward the front.

10. There was even an old camera hidden among the shoes.

11. We lifted the letter from the chest.

12. We carefully opened it with a knife.

13. Inside the envelope was an old, yellow-stained paper.

14. It was written from my grandmother to my father when he was a baby.

15. It said that she would love and protect him until the end.

Pop-Up Phrases

A **prepositional phrase** includes a preposition and an object of the preposition. A prepositional phrase may also contain words that modify the object.

Example: The plane flew **over the baseball park.**

(*Over* is the preposition, *park* is the object of the preposition, and *the* and *baseball* modify *park*.)

Underline the prepositional phrases below. Circle the object of the preposition.

1. Please don't sit on the museum steps.

2. Use caution when walking under the scaffolding.

3. You may pass through the gates.

4. The captain is below the decks.

5. Without a doubt, there will be a thunderstorm tonight.

6. Keep off the grass.

7. No parking between the signs.

8. Your classroom is located down the hall.

9. The ship sailed against the tide.

10. He waited until the last moment.

Daily Skill-Builders Grammar & Usage 5–6
walch.com © 2004 Walch Publishing

Shade the Parts

A **prepositional phrase** includes a preposition and an object of the preposition. A prepositional phrase may also contain words that modify the object.

Example: We slid the paper underneath the teacher's door.
(*Underneath* is the preposition, *door* is the object of the preposition, and *the* and *teacher's* modify *door*.)

Circle the prepositions, write one line under the objects of the prepositions, and write two lines under the words that modify the objects.

1. We traveled underneath three bridges.

2. I forgot my glasses, so I sat toward the front.

3. I found some money on the ground outside the grocery store.

4. We could put a sofa between the two chairs.

5. We always go ice-skating on the pond.

6. I carefully mowed around your flowerbed.

7. Julie, Dan, and Libby tumbled down the small hill.

8. We traveled past the construction site.

9. Many branches fell down during the storm.

10. We bought our lunches at the fair.

Fragment Repair

A **sentence fragment** is not a complete sentence. It is missing important information, such as the subject or the verb (predicate) or both.

Examples: Leaves the room (The subject is missing.)

Justin leaves the room when he's angry. **(complete sentence)**

Not the best idea. (The subject and the verb are missing.)

Cindy's suggestion is not the best idea. **(complete sentence)**

Turn each fragment into a complete sentence. The first one is done for you.

1. Loves to ride ponies.
   Abbey loves to ride ponies.

2. Not my favorite salad.

3. Is bringing ketchup and mayonnaise.

4. Very good.

5. Once in a while.

6. Eats nuts and berries.

7. Washes the vegetables.

8. Very comfortable shoes.

9. Always a good choice.

10. Tries to climb the tree.

Daily Skill-Builders Grammar & Usage 5–6
walch.com © 2004 Walch Publishing

What's Missing?

A sentence **fragment** is not a complete sentence. It is missing important information, such as the subject or the verb (predicate) or both.

Examples: Waters the flowers. **(The subject is missing.)**

Always fun. **(The subject and verb are missing.)**

Write what each sentence below is missing. The first one has been done for you.

1. Never goes.

   _____subject_____

2. Chases the dog.

   _____

3. Not very good.

   _____

4. Yells loudly.

   _____

5. Never bright.

   _____

6. Hot and sticky.

   _____

7. Reels in big fish.

   _____

8. Not my best work.

   _____

9. Sleeps during the day.

   _____

Now, write a complete sentence using each fragment from above.

10. _____

11. _____

12. _____

13. _____

14. _____

15. _____

16. _____

17. _____

18. _____

Catch the Run-Ons!

A **run-on sentence** occurs when two sentences are joined without punctuation or a connecting word.

Example: She bought some milk and she ate some cheese. **(incorrect)**
She bought some milk. She ate some cheese. **(correct)**
She bought some milk, and she ate some cheese. **(correct)**

Fix each run-on sentence below and make it into a complete sentence.

1. The friends played some music and they sang some songs.

2. The dog chewed my sneakers but it didn't touch the pie.

3. The grass is growing quickly so it needs to be mowed more often.

4. My watch fell in the pool but I don't think it is broken.

5. I will buy some lettuce and I will make a salad.

6. We should buy some salsa and we should make some quesadillas.

7. We could play darts or we could play checkers.

8. The lawn mower is loud and it is annoying.

9. I could call you or you could call me.

10. I saw a fire engine but it was far away.

Run Down the Run-Ons

A **run-on sentence** occurs when two sentences are joined without punctuation or a connecting word.

Example: The jar fell off the counter but Margaret caught it. **(incorrect)**

The jar fell off the counter. Margaret caught it. **(correct)**

The jar fell off the counter, but Margaret caught it. **(correct)**

Underline the run-on sentences in the story below. Fill-in the missing punctuation marks.

Finding Lacey

Jason and Patrick watered Mr. McIntyre's plants every time he went away. Mr. McIntyre had a lot of plants in his house and he also had a garden in the backyard. He had roses, daisies, lilies, and peonies in his flower garden and he had tomatoes and cucumbers in his vegetable garden. It usually took Jason and Patrick an hour to finish all of the watering.

Mr. McIntyre had a dog and her name was Lacey. Lacey was a big golden retriever who loved to chase birds but never caught any. Jason and Patrick loved Lacey but they knew they couldn't take her outside to play. Mr. McIntyre had strictly forbidden it. They could ask Mrs. Walker to walk Lacey or they could ask Mr. Spencer to do it. If Lacey got free of her leash she was too fast and too strong for Jason and Patrick to catch.

Jason and Patrick had been at Mr. McIntyre's house for an hour one day when they noticed that the porch door was wide open. They called for Lacey but she didn't come. They hunted everywhere in the house for her. They looked in the basement and they even looked in the attic. Jason said, "If she isn't in the house then she has to be outside."

They looked everywhere outside for Lacey. They looked in the woods and they looked up and down the street. They had almost given up hope when they heard her bark. They ran toward the bark and they found Lacey in the flowerbed. She was stalking a bird that was sitting in the birdbath in the garden. They quietly walked toward her and then they jumped to grab Lacey's collar. Lacey darted through the flowerbed and into the vegetable garden. Lacey tore up all of the flowers and vegetables but they finally got a hold of her. What a mess!

Let Them Run!

A **run-on sentence** occurs when two sentences are joined without punctuation or a connecting word.

> **Example:** I checked underneath all of the desks but I couldn't find my backpack.
> I checked underneath all of the desks, but I couldn't find my backpack.
> **(correct)**
> I checked underneath all of the desks. I couldn't find my backpack.
> **(correct)**

Imagine that you are meeting someone famous whom you admire. You are very nervous and speak very quickly. Write five run-on sentences that you might say to this person. Then correct each of your sentences, using proper punctuation.

Run-on Sentences

1. _____

2. _____

3. _____

4. _____

5. _____

Corrected Run-on Sentences

6. _____

7. _____

8. _____

9. _____

10. _____

Daily Skill-Builders Grammar & Usage 5–6
walch.com © 2004 Walch Publishing

Step 1: Topic Sentence

A **paragraph** is made up of three main parts. The **topic sentence** is at the beginning and states the main idea. The **body** is made up of sentences that support the main idea. The **closing sentence** sums up the message of the paragraph.

Example: Movies may be the best form of entertainment.**(topic sentence)**

(body) { Movies hold the audience's attention with pictures as well as sound. The camera work is so clever that you often feel as if you were there inside the movie. A movie can tell you more about a character than a painting can. A movie shows a person's gestures, and body language is an important part of how we communicate. There's a reason why people love going to the movies! **(closing sentence)**

Think of a topic sentence for the paragraph below. Write it on the first line.

_____

Newspapers often have in-depth stories about important information. Unlike television news, one can learn a lot of details from a newspaper article. Newspapers also cover many topics. They are divided into sections, and each section has several articles. Reporters work hard to find out the facts and to get quotations from people about the issues. Newspapers can be found everywhere. They are on the street, in restaurants, and even on your front stoop! Newspapers may be old-fashioned when compared to the Internet, but they are still a very important source of news.

Step 2: Paragraph

A **paragraph** is made up of three main parts. The **topic sentence** is at the beginning and states the main idea. The **body** is made up of sentences that support the main idea. The **closing sentence** sums up the message of the paragraph.

> **Example:** Vacation is very important for everyone. **(topic sentence)** Vacations often provide a needed break from school and work. Our brains and our bodies need time to rest if they are going to work properly. A vacation gives us the time to relax and to do what we want. Vacations also give us time to have fun. We all need to have fun so that our lives are more enjoyable. So, take a vacation! **(closing sentence)**
>
> **(body)**

Finish the paragraph below. The topic sentence has been written for you.

Too much junk food is not good for you.

_____

_____

_____

_____

_____

_____

_____

_____

_____

_____

Which Type Is It?

Write **declarative**, **interrogative**, **imperative**, or **exclamatory** next to the sentences below. Fill in the missing punctuation marks.

_____ 1. Ouch, a bee is stinging me

_____ 2. Lake Michigan is one of the Great Lakes

_____ 3. Leave me alone

_____ 4. Watch out for the falling brick

_____ 5. Do you want to go to the concert with me

_____ 6. My bedroom is the largest room in our house

_____ 7. Can I see your snail

_____ 8. That is absolutely terrific news

_____ 9. My shoes are in the basement

_____ 10. Look out for the gigantic hole

Write **simple**, **compound**, or **complex** next to the sentences below.

_____ 11. I would love to remain in Hodgetown, but my family is leaving.

_____ 12. There must be an explanation for this.

_____ 13. Because there are too many brownies, we'll have to eat some.

_____ 14. I could bring you some chicken soup, or I could bring you to the doctor.

_____ 15. The players, who were tired and thirsty, went home after the game.

Name It, Create It!

On the first line, label each sentence **D** for declarative, **IM** for imperative, **I** for interrogative, or **E** for exclamatory. On the second line, label each sentence as **S** for simple, **CP** for compound, or **CX** for complex. Write the same *type* of sentence on the line below each sentence.

_____ _____   **1.** A triangle has three sides, and a square has four sides.

_____

_____ _____   **2.** Bring me some more chalk.

_____

_____ _____   **3.** Wow, I can't believe you can do a back flip!

_____

_____ _____   **4.** Because it is raining, I can't ride my bike.

_____

_____ _____   **5.** Look at the huge snake!

_____

_____ _____   **6.** If we see an ice-cream shop, do you want to stop?

_____

_____ _____   **7.** Take the garbage to the side of the road.

_____

_____ _____   **8.** Can I take your picture, or should I take someone else's picture?

_____

_____ _____   **9.** The book is overdue at the library.

_____

_____ _____   **10.** Watch out for the green monsters in the pond!

_____

Daily Skill-Builders Grammar & Usage 5–6
walch.com © 2004 Walch Publishing

Find the Missing Pieces

These sentences are missing something. Add to the **dependent clauses**, **prepositional phrases**, **fragments**, or **run-ons** below, using words and/or punctuation to make a complete sentence.

1. If I lived near the beach.

_____

2. I will watch the children and I will eat my lunch.

_____

3. I already put the peanut butter the cabinet.

_____

4. When I go to Mark's house.

_____

5. I emptied the wastebasket into.

_____

6. I will help you with your homework but you must do the work.

_____

7. The kittens looked identical so I didn't know which was yours.

_____

8. Eats pasta with a spoon.

_____

9. The baseball rolled past the pitcher to the third.

_____

10. Not a good movie.

_____

Search for Clues

Each sentence below is missing either words or punctuation marks. Identify the problem and write it on the line. Write **DP** for dependent clause, **PP** for prepositional phrase, **F** for fragment, or **RO** for run-on Then fix the sentences by using the space above each sentence.

_____ 1. When you see Mr. Radshaw.

_____ 2. Thinks he can lift the big armchair.

_____ 3. I signed the letter and put it the envelope.

_____ 4. I will go skiing the mountain if you come along.

_____ 5. I want to travel to England and I want to meet the queen.

_____ 6. A very good time.

_____ 7. If you want ketchup.

_____ 8. Not a small instrument.

_____ 9. You should read the book or you should watch the movie.

_____ 10. Because there aren't any more seats I'll sit on the floor.

_____ 11. A bat just flew my head!

_____ 12. Waits by the side of the road.

_____ 13. When you go upstairs.

_____ 14. The boy over there who brought us our water is a very good waiter.

_____ 15. Fifteen clowns climbed the car!

Answer Key

PARTS OF SPEECH

Page 1: Places to Go, People to See!

Possible answers:

2. museum 3. musician 4. feelings 5. father 6. hat
7. backpack 8. zoo 9. teacher 10. freedom

Page 2: Catch a Common Noun

Possible answers:

2. patient, health 3. zipper, sleeves 4. toy, house
5. happiness, smiles 6. tent, lake 7. break, cake
8. vegetables, broth 9. woods, farms 10. desks, chairs
11. sand, seagull 12. restaurant, kitchen

Page 3: Go Fly a Kite!

Possible answers:

My Flowerd Kite

Yesterday was a gorgeous summer day. The birds were chirping, the flowers were blooming, and <u>Megan, Rachel, and Sue</u> were playing outside. It was so beautiful that <u>Megan</u> decided it would be a good day to go to <u>Dickson Park</u> and fly a kite. <u>Megan</u> went with Josh and Rachel.

<u>Megan's</u> father had just bought a kite from <u>Roy's Toys</u> for her birthday. It was a large green kite with a long, white tail and a picture of a flower printed on the front. It was so beautiful that she named it <u>Posey</u>. She didn't want <u>Josh</u> and <u>Rachel</u> to play with <u>Posey</u>, but she knew that she had to share it.

<u>Posey</u> flew high. It flew over <u>East Beach Avenue</u>. It flew over <u>Marco's Hardware Store</u>. It flew beside <u>Cape Lighthouse</u>. It flew above the crowds of people at <u>White Sand Beach</u>. It flew above the <u>Atlantic Ocean</u>. <u>Posey</u> kept flying higher and higher and farther away. It flew (Answers will vary)

Page 4: Acting Proper

Possible answers:

2. Harriet Tubman, Eleanor Roosevelt 3. Wyoming, Old Faithful Geyser 4. *New York Times, Arizona Republic*
5. Sammy Sosa, Mia Hamm 6. Ernie's Shoe Shop, Mimi's Donut Shop 7. Alaska, Oklahoma 8. Harry S. Truman, Mr. J. Roberts 9. Saccoppee Elementary School, Rutgers University 10. Philadelphia, San Juan

Page 5: Ups and Downs of Nouns

Common is underlined; proper is not:

1. <u>nurse</u>; Johnson County Hospital, Mrs. Harnett
2. <u>movie</u>; *Spot's Great Adventure* 3. <u>sweater, hat</u>; Sarah's Boutique 4. <u>train, city</u>; Chicago 5. <u>apples, oranges, bananas</u>; Harry's Market 6. <u>jealousy, emotion</u> 7. <u>table,</u>

<u>corner</u>; Mrs. Danby, George 8. <u>waves</u>; Ferry Beach
9. <u>mountain, world</u>; Mount Everest 10. <u>jacket</u>; Seattle
11. <u>break, music</u> 12. <u>band's, album</u>; *Bright Room*

Page 6: Classifying Nouns

1. pilot 2. Aunt Harriet 3. Hinkley Park 4. George
5. Empire State Building 6. ball; C 7. flag; C 8. joy; A
9. sun; C 10. hatred; A 11. spirit; A 12. sled; C
13. surprise; A 14. hammer; C 15. love; A

Page 7: A Flock of Nouns

1. class 2. team 3. litter 4. herd 5. batch 6. family
7. pack 8. singers 9. stars 10. geese 11. scouts, police, soldiers, baboons, or kangaroos 12. fish or porpoises
13. cards 14. ants, soldiers, or caterpillars

Page 8: A Bunch of Balloons

1. bouquet 2. pack 3. gaggle 4. bunch 5. fleet 6. staff
7. litter 8. batch 9. class 10. colony 11. band 12. grove
13. audience 14. array 15. cluster

Page 9: Beach Collections

1. band 2. flock 3. class 4. colony 5. bouquet 6. family
7. fleet 8. team 9. forest 10. herd

Page 10: Plural Noun Stars

1. shoes 2. cats 3. bananas 4. crayons 5. surprises
6. papers 7. plants 8. phones 9. computers 10. pirates
11. eyes 12. floors 13. astronauts 14. stages 15. games

Page 11: Plural Pops

1. patches 2. taxes 3. dresses 4. rashes 6. watches
8. glasses 10. waltzes

Page 12: More Than One

2. benches 3. cameras 4. malls 5. dresses 6. witches
7. patches 8. cups 9. peaches 10. classes 11. desks
12. gardens 13. cars 14. foxes 15. baskets

Page 13: Change Y to I

2. families 3. mysteries 4. poppies 5. ponies 6. policies
7. assemblies 8. disabilities 9. communities 10. dairies
11. comedies 12. cherries

Page 14: A Flock of V's and a Bunch of O's

1. scarves 2. roofs 3. lives 4. wives 5. wharves 6. cliffs
7. potatoes 8. radios 9. dominoes 10. patios 11. tomatoes
12. studios

Page 15: Spot the Difference

Irregular plural nouns are bold:

1. **children** 2. geese 3. hats 4. **mice** 5. chairs 6. **deer**
7. calculators 8. **people** 9. **men** 10. ribbons 11. **women**
12. **oxen**

Page 16: Yours or Mine?

1. puppy's 2. Charlie's 3. girl's 4. lady's 5. fox's
6. Anthony's 7. country's 8. teacher's 9. grandfather's
10. carpenter's 11. friend's 12. cook's 13. duckling's
14. scientist's 15. writer's

Page 17: Whose Is It?

1. children's 2. actors' 3. people's 4. parents' 5. geese's
6. ducks' 7. fawns' 8. deer's 9. birds' 10. mice's
11. women's 12. players'

Page 18: Are They Together?

2. Casey's 3. Miguel's and Juan's 4. Mrs. Humphrey's and
Mr. Bartlett's 5. dad's 6. Clark's 7. Lewis's and Clark's
8. nurse's 9. coach's and the player's 10. Lucas's
11. Jonathan's 12. Rob's and Molly's

Page 19: Pair Them Up!

1. corp. 2. ave. 3. cent. 4. inc. 5. gal. 6. pop. 7. assn.
8. capt. 9. univ. 10. div. 11. sec. 12. dept. 13. gov.
14. st. 15. vol. 16. subj. 17. atty. 18. ex.
19–20. Answers will vary.

Page 20: Shorten Them!

1. VT (or Vt.) 2. Dr. 3. Ave. 4. Wed. 5. NE (or Nebr.)
6. Oct. 7. HI 8. Blvd. 9. Sr. 10. D.D.S. 11. Rev.
12. Sen. 13. Prof. 14. NY or N.Y. 15. Lt.

Page 21: Measure Up!

1. lb. 2. c. 3. ml 4. gr. 5. yd. 6. in. 7. pt. 8. ac. 9. qt.
10. rpm 11. gal. 12. mph 13. fl. oz. 14. mm 15. m

Page 22: Athletic Actions

1. kicked 2. threw 3. bounced 4. tosses 5. stands
6. swings 7. catches 8. hit 9. run 10. flip 11. jumped
12. fold

Page 23: Follow the Action!

1. hammered 2. shuffled 3. hopped 4. fixed 5. sings
6. brought 7. grow 8. fell 9. sprayed 10. burned
11. rings 12. batted 13. ride 14. blew 15. picked

Page 24: Take Action!

Possible answers:

1. walk 2. climbed 3. pulled 4. ate 5. roared 6. stand
7. blow
8–10. A firefighter sprays water on burning buildings. A
firefighter drives a fire engine. A firefighter climbs ladders.
A firefighter carries people out of burning homes. A
firefighter searches buildings for people. A firefighter saves
many lives.

Page 25: Connect the Caboose

1. smell 2. appears 3. sounds 4. tastes 5. am 6. turn
7. being 8. remain 9. were 10. feels 11. grow 12. is
13. looks 14. are 15. seems

Page 26: What's Missing?

1. The homemade ice cream **tastes** delicious. 2. The
bananas will **turn** brown if you leave them there. 3. My
scooter **is** very old. 4. The runner **appeared** very tired at
the end of the race. 5. The new car **looks** shiny in the
sunlight. 6. I **am** excited to go to a foreign country.
7. The speaker **seems** nervous. 8. The stale cookies **feel**
hard. 9. The tadpoles will **become** frogs. 10. The players
were tired after the long game.

Page 27: I'm Late!

1. should 2. had 3. did 4. would 5. were 6. must 7. will
8. may 9. am 10. could 11. can 12. shall

Page 28: Helping Hands

1. may 2. will 3. have 4. am 5. can 6. could 7. are
8. should 9. must 10. has

Possible answers:

11. I would love to have a lifetime supply of noodles. 12. I
can certainly carry those bags. 13. I could ask someone for
directions. 14. I am going to take a short nap. 15. I think
that the boys should have said goodbye.

Page 29: To Link or to Help?

Linking verb; subject; noun or adjective in predicate:
1. sounded; music; terrific 2. feel; oranges; soft 3. am; I;
surprised 4. seems; substitute; strict 5. are; moms; cooks
6. tastes; tomatoes; sweet 7. looks; road; slippery 8. are;
They; kind 9. turns; hair; blond 10. became; aunt; lawyer
Helping verb; main verb:
11. must; feed 12. should; buy 13. can; recite 14. may;
bring 15. would; make 16. am; playing 17. has; given
18. could; give 19. is; helping 20. will; write

Page 30: Past, Present, and Future

1. will read, future 2. chases, present 3. went, past
4. listens, present 5. protected, past 6. will meet, future
7. looks, present 8. guess, present 9. ate, past 10. grabbed,
past 11. dig, present 12. crawled, past 13. will attend,
future 14. chewed, past 15. will have, future

Page 31: Time Travel

1. mowed, will mow 2. climb, climbed 3. move, will
move 4. live, lived 5. skated, will skate

Page 32: A Trip to the Desert

1. drive 2. visit 3. see 4. are 5. like 6. sets 7. remember
8. saw 9. traveled 10. felt 11. were 12. was 13. thought
14. stared 15. said 16. will go 17. will come 18. will be
19. will bring 20. will make 21. will buy 22. will purchase
23. will be

Page 33: Who or What?

Action verb, direct object:
1. tied, bow 2. sang, tunes 3. drove, boat 4. give, stickers
5. likes, flowers 6. traced, pictures 7. sells, sandglass

8. races, cars 9. stuck, note 10. planted; tomatoes, cucumbers, radishes 11. checked, throat 12. tell, stories 13. made, noises 14. carves, statues 15. sniffed, skunk

Page 34: Direct Me to Your Object
1. bikes, direct object (d.o.) 2. fireflies, d.o. 3. bubbles, d.o. 4. tree 5. boat, d.o. 6. pants 7. ear 8. rocks, d.o. 9. back 10. cherries, d.o.

Page 35: I Object!
Action verb, indirect object:
1. informed, us 2. gave, Cindy 3. showed, us 4. told, crowd 5. left, Jane 6. brought, us 7. told, me 8. sent, me 9. wrote, friend 10. promised, runners 11. caught, me 12. read, me 13. made, us 14. played, me 15. promised, Janet

Page 36: What's Your Profession?
Possible answers; indirect objects are italicized:
1. us some hot chocolate. (*us*) 2. my father the good news about his health. (*father*) 3. him some scrambled eggs. (*him*) 4. the jurors his closing speech. (*jurors*) 5. Mr. Henson a complete report. (*Mr. Henson*) 6. me a new house. (*me*) 7. new songs to the audience. (*audience*) 8. you a great picture. (*you*) 9. us a new lesson on grammar. (*us*) 10. you the wrong battery. (*you*)

Page 37: To Whom It May Concern
Direct object, indirect object:
1. wishes, me 2. cake, Josh 3. story, Derek 4. ketchup, me 5. invitation, Susan 6. wildflowers, Mom 7. plants, Louisa 8. time, us 9. patches, me 10. dinner, us

Page 38: Point Out the Irregulars
1. irreg., saw 2. irreg., ate 3. reg., climbed 4. irreg., fought 5. irreg., dove; reg., dived 6. reg., competed 7. irreg., swung 8. irreg., woke 9. irreg., blew 10. reg., revealed 11. reg., screamed 12. reg., insisted 13. reg., whispered 14. irreg., began 15. irreg., stole 16. irreg., shone; reg., shined 17. reg., suggested 18. irreg., shook 19. reg., defeated 20. reg., avoided

Page 39: Pick Out the Irregulars
1. burst (irreg.) 2. rang (irreg.); ringed (reg.) 3. observed (reg.) 4. forced (reg.) 5. froze (irreg.) 6. disregarded (reg.) 7. knew (irreg.) 8. bit (irreg.) 9. wore (irreg.) 10. demanded (reg.) 11. effected (reg.) 12. sank or sunk (irreg.) 13. hoisted (reg.) 14. came (irreg.) 15. hid (irreg.)

Page 40: Mixed-Up Verbs
2. throw 3. sleeps 4. sit 5. smells 6. grows 7. lose 8. glows 9. pick 10. mows

Page 41: Mix and Match
1. hibernate 2. races 3. melt 4. skate 5. treat 6. burns 7. falls 8. fly 9. bakes 10. protects 11. slides 12. hide
Sentences will vary.

Page 42: Reach an Agreement
1. gives 2. think, is 3. comes, are 4. buys, use 5. glows 6. shine 7. glide 8. love 9. walks, ride 10. want
11–12. Answers will vary.

Page 43: Tricky Transitives
1. T, ball 2. T, television 3. NT 4. NT 5. T, pictures 6. NT 7. T, fingers 8. T, ice cream 9. NT 10. NT 11. T, flowers 12. T, winner 13. T, bananas 14. NT 15. T, picture

Page 44: Make It Transitive
Possible answers:
2. <u>conducts</u> the band 3. <u>blew</u> loud music 4. <u>beat</u> the drums 5. <u>reads</u> music 6. <u>sings</u> songs 7. <u>performed</u> "Over the Rainbow" 8. <u>hearing</u> concerts 9. <u>hum</u> the songs 10. <u>play</u> the flute 11. <u>is practicing</u> "Beat the Drums Slowly" 12. <u>carry</u> their instruments

Page 45: It All Ends Here
1. b. in our neighbor's garden 2. a. past a large group of people 3. a. to every house in the neighborhood 4. a. after I finish doing this 5. b. into the room 6. b. when we dance 7. a. very slowly sometimes 8. b. before I came 9. b. under the bed 10. a. off the coast of Mexico

Page 46: Intransitive Verbs
The following numbers contain intransitive verbs:
1, 2, 4, 5, 7, 9, 10, 12
13–18. Sentences will vary.

Page 47: On the Farm
1. T, cows 2. T, noise 3. I 4. T, dirt 5. I 6. T, tractor 7. I 8. I 9. I 10. T, vegetables 11. I 12. T, barn 13. T, calves 14. I 15. T, farm

Page 48: On to Adjectives
Adjective, noun described:
1. big, bag 2. dangerous, bears 3. kind, gentleman 4. large, mouths 5. talented, dancer 6. fastest, runner 7. best, camp 8. rare, jewels 9. beautiful, flowers 10. hot, pavement 11. crowded, subway 12. brick, wall 13. new, car 14. bright, stars 15. small, tent

Page 49: A Room of Adjectives
1. brown 2. comfortable 3. large 4. comfortable 5. white, gray 6. noisy 7. new 8. ten 9. tall 10. Harmless

Page 50: Adjectives That Compare
Possible answers:
1. taller 2. more talented 3. greener 4. more immature

5. colder 6. deeper 7. redder 8. hotter 9. faster
10. louder 11. sharpest 12. loudest 13. messiest 14.
prettiest 15. nicest 16. healthiest 17. most delicious 18.
scariest 19. longest 20. largest

Page 51: Scrambled Adjectives
1. hottest 2. faster 3. biggest 4. taller 5. wetter
6. brightest 7. sweeter 8. hungrier 9. reddest 10. freshest
11. rounder 12. crispier 13. lighter 14. cutest
15. shortest

Page 52: Adjective Articles
1. a 2. an 3. a 4. a 5. an 6. an 7. a 8. an 9. a
10. an 11. a 12. an 13. The 14. a 15. the 16. the 17. a
18. a 19. a 20. the

Page 53: Point to It
1. a 2. the, doughnut 3. a 4. an 5. the, sundial 6. the,
dog 7. The, papers 8. a 9. an 10. the, book 11. the,
hammer 12. an 13. the, kitten 14. a 15. the, circus

Page 54: At the Carnival
1. loudly 2. quickly 3. happily 4. silently 5. eagerly
6. softly 7. brightly 8. accidentally 9. secretly
10. rarely 11. skillfully 12. carefully 13. tightly
14. safely 15. surely

Page 55: Adverb Olympics
1. first 2. daily 3. briefly 4. last 5. yearly 6. recently
7. rarely 8. temporarily 9. sooner 10. frequently
11. usually 12. yesterday 13. previously 14. instantly
15. quickly

Page 56: To What Degree?
1. completely 2. very 3. extremely 4. quite 5. too
6. unbelievably 7. amazingly 8. totally 9. certainly
10. surely 11. never 12. always 13. enough 14. little
15. quite

Page 57: Summer Camp
1. always 2. quickly 3. usually 4. briefly 5. very
6. extremely 7. near 8. daily 9. quite 10. often
11. Sometimes 12. eagerly 13. completely 14. never
15. really

Page 58: Out to Dinner
1. It 2. They 3. We 4. He 5. It 6. She 7. It 8. We 9. I
10. It 11. He 12. It 13. We 14. It 15. they

Page 59: Subject Switch!
1. I went to the zoo with Tara and Lindsey. 2. I like mint
chocolate chip ice cream. 3. We fell out of the canoe
when Josh stood up. 4. We bring him flowers in the
hospital. 5. You buy the red socks with the white stripes.
6. You are building a sand castle with Donna. 7. Do you
like my posters? 8. You will love the five pounds of
spaghetti I made. 9. She likes to visit the dentist!

10. She raises beautiful monarch butterflies. 11. They are
coming to my birthday party. 12. They fill up the
auditorium.

Page 60: A Trip to the Museum
2. it 3. him 4. us 5. it, her 6. them 7. them 8. me
9. them 10. her 11. me 12. her 13. her 14. it 15. it, it

Page 61: Fill in the Objects
Possible answers; pronouns are underlined:
2. Would you lend me your pink shoes? 3. The driver
brought us to the front door. 4. He will give us a lesson.
5. I can see you hiding behind the bush. 6. He baked you
a pumpkin pie. 7. They heard you from the other room.
8. We will give you a thousand lollipops. 9. We noticed
him standing by the window. 10. I sang him my favorite
song. 11. We lifted them onto the truck. 12. I picked
them some roses.

Page 62: Possessive Pronouns
1. their 2. our 3. my 4. his 5. your 6. theirs 7. mine
8. its 9. hers 10. his

Page 63: Reflexives in the Mirror
1. Jena always buys herself gifts on vacation. 2. Mike likes
to pat himself on the back after a good game. 3. Aisha
and Kim laugh themselves silly. 4. We helped ourselves
to second helpings. 5. Malik drives himself to work in the
morning. 6. I like to tell myself that it will be okay.
7. The dog licked itself before going to bed. 8. They each
gave themselves a bonus. 9. You will have to find yourself
a new partner. 10. We accidentally put ourselves in
danger.

Page 64: Possessive or Reflexive?
1. mine, P 2. his, P 3. ourselves, R 4. its, P 5. theirs, P
6. himself, R 7. her, P 8. themselves, R 9. his, P
10. herself, R 11. change *their* to *theirs* 12. change *ours*
to *ourselves* 13. correct 14. correct 15. change *himself*
to *his*

Page 65: Me, Myself, and I
1. his 2. herself 3. ours 4. their 5. himself 6. theirs
7. myself 8. its 9. my 10. themselves 11. yours
12. themselves

Page 66: Find the Antecedent
1. Artists 2. family 3. Raspberries 4. Natalia 5. Jack
6. house 7. Terry 8. Rashid 9. group 10. rabbit

Page 67: Pronoun-Antecedent Match
Pronoun, antecedent:
1. it, bike 2. they, parents 3. we, Sharon and I 4. you,
Pedro 5. she, Jill 6. she, Anna 7. you, Amanda and Joey
8. he, Manuel 9. they, friends 10. it, skateboard

Page 68: Arrows and Antecedents

Possible answers:

2. **Mr. Hammerstein** left when **he** saw that we had already finished. 3. **Nicole** gave me her homework before **she** left. 4. **My little sister and I** like to eat a cookie before **we** go to bed. 5. **The flight attendant** worked quickly when we asked **her** for some soda. 6. **The carpenters** built exactly what we asked **them** to build. 7. **The waiter** looked surprised when we gave **him** a large tip. 8. **Ivan, you** shouldn't leave the back door open. 9. **The band and I** were late because it took **us** an hour to pack up the instruments. 10. **Jamal and Dale, you** should make at least four loaves of bread.

Page 69: A Few Indefinite Pronouns

1. Cross out *Nobody*; possibly replace with *Henry* 2. Nothing 3. Something 4. Few 5. Cross out *Everybody*; possibly replace with *My family* 6. Several 7. Cross out *Both*; possibly replace with *This* 8. Either 9. Cross out *somebody*; possibly replace with *Timothy* 10. Much 11. One 12. Some, none 13. Cross out *Anybody*; possibly replace with *My friends* 14. All 15. neither

Page 70: It's All Relative

1. whose 2. whom 3. whatever 4. which 5. who 6. whichever 7. that 8. who 9. whatever 10. Whoever 11. what 12. whichever 13. which 14. whose 15. that

Page 71: Conjunctions Make Sense!

1. We like to dance **and** sing in the rain. 2. My mother broke her leg, **but** she is still in good spirits. 3. We could have our picnic on the hill **or** at the park. 4. I didn't see him **nor** do I want to see him. 5. I got a card **and** a new bike for my birthday. 6. We should take the clothes out of the rain, **or** they will get wet. 7. We swam in the ocean, **and** we built sand castles. 8. My father is away, **so** you can't see him right now. 9. Ruby doesn't like to shop, **yet** she still comes with me to the mall. 10. I want to see my cousin in Texas, **so** I am going there next week.

Page 72: Conjunction Pair-Up

1. Neither/nor 2. Both/and 3. Whether/or 4. As/so 5. Not only/ but/ also 6. Either/or 7. Both/and 8. Neither/nor 9. Not only/ but/ also 10. Whether/or

Page 73: Catch a Dependent Clause

2. I have to take my medicine so that my body heals. 3. I get nervous when I fly on planes. 4. The baby will cry unless she has her pacifier. 5. I found my shoes where I left them. 6. I went swimming before I ate dinner. 7. My sister chews gum while she talks on the phone. 8. The little drummer acts as though he was in a band. 9. I haven't seen the ocean since my visit last October. 10. The music was hurting my head, so I turned it off.

Page 74: Inject Life in These Sentences!

Possible answers:

1. Wow! 2. Look! 3. Ouch, 4. Unbelievable! 5. Fantastic! 6. Well, 7. Yum! 8. Oh no, 9. Hey, 10. Gosh, 11. Great! 12. Wait, 13. That's terrible! 14. Sorry! 15. Terrific!

Page 75: Create the Mood

Possible answers:

1. Look! 2. Great, 3. Hey, 4. Oh no! 5. Watch out! 6. Wow! 7. That's terrible! 8. Ouch, 9. Super! 10. Sorry! 11. Fantastic! 12. Wait, 13. Gosh, 14. Excellent! 15. Look out!

Page 76: A Picture's Worth 1,000 Words

Possible answers:

2. A bird flew **beside** the balloon. 3. Two people waited below **on** the ground. 4. The girl waved **to** those in the balloon. 5. Two people traveled **in** the balloon. 6. The balloon floated **over** the people. 7. One person in the balloon pointed **at** the girl. 8. One person in the balloon pointed **up to** the clouds. 9. A string is hanging **down** from the balloon. 10. The balloon floated **toward** another town.

Page 77: Position the Players

1. near 2. into 3. of 4. toward 5. behind 6. under 7. on 8. between 9. past 10. at 11. inside 12. over 13. through 14. across 15. beside

Page 78: Nouns by Number

Possible answers:

1. Turner Fair 2. St. 3. food 4. herd, flock 5. mother's 6. blankets, lamps 7. Jr. 8. Dr. 9. Dr., tickets 10. family's 11. Finnegan's Bakery 12. bouquet 13. mother's, Lily and Barton's Flowers 14. artist, Jessica Zorith 15. Jessica, whiskers

Page 79: Test Your Noun Skills

1. possessive 2. collective 3. common, common 4. proper 5. collective 6. proper 7. possessive 8. abbreviation 9. abbreviation 10. collective 11. wives, scarves 12. children 13. deer, mice 14. wharves 15. chairs, tables 16. potatoes 17. pools 18. studios 19. teams 10. lives

Page 80: Verse Yourself in Verbs

1. action 2. linking 3. linking 4. helping 5. action 6. linking 7. helping 8. action 9. linking 10. helping 11. intransitive 12. transitive 13. transitive 14. intransitive 15. transitive

Page 81: Verbs to the Test

1. d.o.: dollars, i.o.: charity 2. d.o.: chocolates, i.o.: us 3. d.o.: postcard, i.o.: him 4. d.o.: brownies, i.o.: neighbors

5. d.o.: kiss, i.o.: girl 6. irregular 7. irregular 8. regular
9. irregular 10. regular 11. shipped 12. will sing 13. sat
14. plays 15. cooks

Page 82: What Is Being Described?

1. adv: quickly, describes *walked*; adj: busy, describes *street*
2. adv: very, describes *nice*; adj: nice, describes *people*
3. adj: shy, describes *He*; adj.: new, describes *people* 4. adj.:
sweet, describes *tea* 5. adv: quickly, describes *skated* 6. adj:
large, describes *room* 7. adj: beautiful, describes *shade*
8. adj: crooked, describes *one* 9. adv: completely, describes
forgot; adj: homework, describes *paper* 10. adj: bright, new,
describe *lamp;* adv: perfectly, describes *works* 11. adj: gold,
describes *medal* 12. adv: too, describes *large;* adj.: large,
describes *burrito* 13. adv: softly, describes *buzzes* 14. adj:
thirsty, describes *I*; adj: salty potato, describe *chips*
15. adv: hurriedly, describes *ran*

Page 83: Pronoun Review

1. We, subject 2. mine, possessive 3. who, relative
4. Nobody, indefinite 5. themselves, reflexive 6. us,
object 7. his, possessive 8. someone, indefinite 9. you,
subject 10. me, object 11. theirs, possessive 12. who,
relative 13. most, indefinite 14. our, possessive
15. himself, reflexive

Page 84: Look! Review Parts of Speech!

Possible answers:

1. Ouch 2. and 3. Neither/nor 4. or 5. Wow 6. Hey
7. so 8. Both/and 9. and 10. Look 11. under 12. inside
13. on 14. down 15. toward

CAPITALIZATION

Page 85: Memorial Day

Capitalize the first word of each sentence, the holidays,
the months, and the days of the week.

Page 86: Capitalize Correctly

Capitalize the following numbered words:

1, 2, 4, 5, 7, 8, 9, 11, 12, 14, 15, 16

Page 87: A Proper Noun Picnic

1. We went to Fort Dixon Park for a picnic last Saturday.
2. The park is near Lake Higgins, which is not far from
Lake Magnum. 3. My favorite park is Central Park in New
York City, New York. 4. There are also some very nice
parks in San Francisco and Quebec City, too. 5. I went
on a picnic with Aunt Harriet and my friend Jordan.
6. Jordan's little brother Harry was going to come, but his
mom wouldn't let him. 7. We brought lots of food from
Sam's Deli. 8. I brought my favorite book called The
Adventures of Silly Sue. 9. Jordan brought his favorite CD,
called Walking on the Clouds. 10. We read books, listened
to music, and gazed at Mount Fairfield in the distance.

Page 88: Which Ones Don't Belong?

1. walk, bouquet 2. daisies, lilies, house 3. shop, market
4. meat, squash 5. friend 6. tonsils 7. throat, ice cream
8. kind, ice cream 9. groceries 10. door

Page 89: My Uncle Max

1. Europe, Paris, France 2. China, Spain 3. Hong Kong,
Beijing, China, Barcelona, Spain 4. Africa 5. Asia,
Australia 6. Norway, Japan 7. Georgia, Maine, Idaho
8. Canada, British Columbia, Quebec 9. North America,
Miami, Toronto, Chicago 10. Detroit, Houston, Texas

Page 90: Pack Your Bags!

Possible answers:

Planets: Pluto, Mars, Jupiter **Continents:** Antarctica,
Australia, South America **Countries:** Brazil, Canada,
Japan **States and Provinces:** British Columbia, Oregon,
Minnesota **Cities:** Los Angeles, Montreal, Dallas
Counties: Orange County, Washington County,
Cumberland County

Page 91: Family Tree

Possible answers:

1. My mother will come to the beach with us. 2. Mother
doesn't like to swim. 3. My father built that tree house.
4. I heard Father say that he'll build another one. 5. Your
aunt brought the pie. 6. Aunt Ruth lives in California.
7. His uncle picked him up from school. 8. I think that
Uncle is leaving tomorrow. 9. My grandfather loves
pistachios and cashews. 10. Grandfather Jones lives in
Vermont. 11. I saw your grandmother at the market.
12. Grandmother made me these mittens.

Page 92: Cap It!

1. I am going to Santa Fe, New Mexico with Father and
Mother tomorrow. 2. We ate lunch with Uncle Luke at a
little café in Paris. 3. The best place to go in Asia would
be either China or Japan. 4. My grandfather and I took
Interstate 45 to Yellowstone National Park. 5. Many
people fly during Christmas and Thanksgiving vacations.
6. If Valentine's Day is on a Friday this year, my father will
take Mother on a trip. 7. We are going to sail on the
Pacific Ocean for the whole month of May and a part of
June. 8. I told Uncle Malcolm not to expect us at his
home for Kwanza this year. 9. Maybe I will go to Mars or
Pluto when I'm older. 10. Grandfather Rivera took us to
the Museum of Natural History in New York City. 11. We
drove across the Rocky Mountains on our way to Moab,
Utah. 12. My sister and I saw the Great Barrier Reef with
our father. 13. Next Monday we should take a trip across
the Green Mountains in Vermont. 14. If Mom would let
me, I'd eat chocolate ice cream every Friday, Saturday, and
Sunday. 15. Our whole family is going to be in Ireland on
St. Patrick's Day.

PUNCTUATION

Page 93: Family Reunion

Only 5 and 10 do not take periods.
1. statement 2. request 3. statement 4. statement
6. statement 7. command 8. request 9. request
11. command 12. statement 13–15. Sentences will vary.

Page 94: A Trip to the Moon

1. Are there any mountains on the moon? 2. I wonder
what Earth looks like from the moon. 3. Can you run on
the moon? 4. What color is the ground? 5. One square
mile on the moon has 500 (?) craters, I think. 6. If you'd
like, I'll buy you a moon rock. 7. Will I be able to go to
the moon when I am older? 8. Other solar systems have
moons, too, right? 9. I wonder if people will ever live on
the moon. 10. Would you go to the moon if you could?
11–15. Sentences will vary.

Page 95: Famous Author Interview

Possible answers:

Famous Author: Roald Dahl 1. How long does it take
you to write a book? 2. How did you think of the idea for
Charlie and the Chocolate Factory? 3. Did you want to be
a writer when you were young? 4. Who are your favorite
authors? 5. Which was your favorite book to write? 6. Do
you have any advice for young writers? 7. You grew up in
England, right? 8. Do you like the movie Charlie and the
Chocolate Factory? 9. You wrote your first children's story
called The Gremlins (?) when you were young. 10. You
wrote either Matilda or Tuck Everlasting, didn't you?

Page 96: Jazz Them Up!

Place an exclamation point after the following:
1, 2, 4, 5, 7, 8, 10, 11, 12
13–16. Answers will vary.

Page 97: Sweet Tooth!

Possible answers:

1. Sweet! 2. I love candy! 3. Licorice is my favorite!
4. Oh no! 5. I ate my bed! 6. The house will melt
if it rains! 7. The floor tastes great! 8. My pillow is a
marshmallow! 9. Happy Eating! 10. The door tastes great
with chocolate! 11. Be careful! 12. The floor is sticky!

Page 98: A Day at the Fair

Place an exclamation point after the following:
1, 2, 3, 4, 8, 9, 12, 14, 15

Place a period after the following:
5, 6, 7, 10, 11, 13

Page 99: Make a Series!

Possible answers:

1. roll over, play dead, and fetch sticks. 2. apples, bananas,
and strawberries. 3. swim in the ocean, walk in the sand,
and collect shells. 4. ice skate, build snow forts, and throw
snow balls. 5. swordfish, bluefish, and tuna. 6. bridges,
houses, and office buildings. 7. papers, clothing, and
magazines. 8. a new coat, a new pair of sneakers, and a
video game. 9. chickens, goats, and sheep. 10. New York,
Phoenix, and Seattle.

Page 100: Can You Switch Them?

1. The large colonial house at the end of the road is mine.
2. Sandy and Teresa will bring their large, pink backpacks.
3. Mike likes to take long, boring drives through the
mountains. 4. My family had big, juicy burgers for dinner.
5. The gardener planted fragrant, red flowers around the
house. 6. The long fiction book you gave me was terrific!
7. The sticky, squishy strawberry syrup is making a mess!
8. Please take my annoying baby brother with you.
9. The loud, shiny trumpets were my favorite. 10. The
hot summer sun was too bright to look at. 11. The nice
substitute teacher let us go outside for recess. 12. He is
the captain of a big, red fishing boat. 13. It was a windy,
bitter, raw day. 14. The cute, little robin sings to me every
morning. 15. I don't know anyone who dislikes gooey
chocolate brownies.

Page 101: Say It Again!

1. My brother, the best player on the team, received
the award. 2. My aunt, a great cook, makes the best
quesadillas in town. 3. Mrs. Hutchins, a new teacher,
didn't know where to take the class. 4. We went to Fort
Larrame Park, my favorite park, for a picnic lunch. 5. We
took a train, the Pacific Railroad, to Mexico. 6. My rabbit,
the highest jumper in the East, always escapes from its
cage. 7. We love to eat chocolate-covered strawberries,
our favorite dessert, on hot summer days. 8. Joe lives on
Scammon Street, a quiet side street, with his three best
friends. 9. Nick, a very funny guy, keeps us laughing all
day long. 10. Mr. Ortega, our neighbor across the street,
always says hello. 11. Coach Greely, the girls' soccer
coach, is a very strict man. 12. We are going to Santigula,
a small island, for vacation. 13. I want some papaya, a
tropical fruit, for breakfast. 14–15. Sentences will vary.

Page 102: Sentence Workout

Possible answers:

1. He ran forty miles, so he is very tired. 2. We could go
to the movie theater, or we could rent a DVD and stay at
home. 3. I ate fifty chocolate pieces, and then I felt really
sick. 4. I like to look at squid in the aquarium, but I don't
want to eat one for dinner. 5. We went to the mall and the
grocery store after dinner. 6. We will go to either Sam's
camp or Hiroshi's house. 7. I have never seen a rattlesnake,
nor do I want to see one. 8. My grandmother has a house
on the beach, so she goes there for the summer. 9. We will

eat spinach, and we will love it. 10. He remembered to lock the house but forgot to bring the key.

Page 103: The Three C Rule
1. My mother broke her ankle, so she is on crutches.
2. The paper flew off the desk and landed on the counter.
3. We will finish cooking, but we can't do the dishes.
4. Kevin drove a bumper car, and then he rode the roller coaster. 5. We will go to either Alaska or Mexico for vacation. 6. I have never been camping, nor do I want to go camping. 7. We should bring our umbrellas, for we will get wet if it rains. 8. The tickets will be sold quickly, so come early. 9. My father complains about shoveling, yet he refuses to let me help. 10. We may be there tomorrow but maybe not.

Possible answers:

11. we don't have enough money. 12. I will open my presents. 13. he called his mom. 14. I will run track.
15. does she want to talk about it.

Page 104: Yes, No, and Well
1. Janet said, "Well, maybe it wouldn't be such a great idea." 2. I am feeling well today. 3. No, I don't think we should swim after eating. 4. My mom always says "no" when I ask if I can play inside. 5. There are no raisins in my lunch box today. 6. Yes, we should definitely bring sunscreen to the beach. 7. Well, it would be easier to go if we had a ride. 8. I answered "yes" to all of the questions.
9. No, maybe Grandpa isn't feeling well today. 10. Yes, I would love to come with you.

Page 105: Places, Everyone!
Possible answers:

1. Shannon, move the lights to the other side of the stage.
2. Please, Carlos, don't forget your lines. 3. Wendy, lean to the right when you say that. 4. Debbie, use more emotion in your speech. 5. Sonia, think of something really sad when you say that. 6. Anna, skip across the stage after Carlos reads his line. 7. Megan, try not to laugh during this scene. 8. Please, Tom, don't chew gum when you're speaking. 9. Anita, don't speak so quickly.
10. Richard, please find a costume that has a sword.

Page 106: Give Me a Break!
1. <u>Before the storm</u>, I was playing with my dog. 2. <u>With this degree of confusion</u>, I'll buy a map. 3. I ate two hot dogs <u>during the baseball game</u>. 4. <u>Until the end of the storm</u>, no one can say a word. 5. The fox ran <u>in front of the bike</u>. 6. I put all of my notebooks <u>on my desk</u>.
7. <u>Except for the last three words</u>, I memorized the entire poem. 8. I found a rabbit's hole <u>beside the tree in the backyard</u>. 9. <u>Without my science notes</u>, I couldn't do my homework. 10. <u>Up to the last month of school</u>, I had never missed a day.

Possible answers:

11. his first semester of graduate school, 12. our trip to the ice-cream shop, 13. his work in sculpting, 14. a picture in a magazine,

Page 107: Let Them Catch a Breath!
1. I had bacon, tomatoes, turkey, onions, and cucumbers in my salad. 2. If you go to the mall, would you buy me a CD? 3. We could buy Mom a gift, or we could make her one. 4. Keisha, would you please come over here? 5. Yes, I should have thought of that before. 6. My grandfather, who was a captain on a fishing boat, loves the ocean. 7. I like your bright, shiny bracelet. 8. The frog jumped onto the lily pad, and it caught a fly. 9. Jerry, toss the ball to Patrick next time. 10. My favorite book, the one that you lent to me, is lost. 11. We packed lunches, put the boat on the car, and drove to the lake. 12. I don't like that slimy, sticky thing on my plate. 13. Well, maybe I should bring the clothes inside. 14. Mr. Kim, may we please go outside for recess? 15. Until we know that it is safe, we shouldn't travel there.

Page 108: C Is for Cookie
1. Lucas' cookie is sitting on his desk. 2. Lucas' sister's cookie is in her mouth. 3. One cookie is in William's pocket. 4. Another cookie is in Ross's drawer. 5. Mrs. Phillips saw Casey's cookie on his chair. 6. Brad said that he would grab a cookie after Rufus' cookie was eaten.
7. Rufus said that he would wait until Melissa's sister had eaten her cookie. 8. Melissa's sister was waiting for Lucas' mother to bring some milk. 9. Lucas' mother is now running up the stairs to Mrs. Phillips' classroom.
10. Lucas' mother's legs are short; so one person will have to wait for a cookie.
The cookie belongs to Brad.

Page 109: Make It Theirs
1. The children's museum opens on Friday. 2. Those boys' desks are very dirty. 3. The women's locker is down the hall on the right. 4. Ryan's, Catherine's, and Isabel's presents will be here tomorrow. 5. I wish that I had seen Erin and Sara's presentation. 6. All of the teachers' children are coming to the picnic. 7. The cats' paws look like they were dunked in mud. 8. That should be the entire class's decision. 9. All of the chickens' eggs are orange. 10. The band's concert will be on Wednesday.
11. Sharon's watches are on the couch. 12. The nurses' patients will be moved to a different wing.

Page 110: The Amazing Apostrophe
1. George got A's and B's on his report card. 2. I am in the class of '05, and my brother is in the class of '08. 3. We want to take a vacation in '07. 4. My mom can't tell the 8's from the 3's without her glasses. 5. I was yellin' 'cause

it was really painful. 6. My aunt was born during the blizzard of '88. 7. All of the 5's and 2's are missing from the deck of cards. 8. Someone crossed out all of the O's on the sign. 9. I got a big bump, but I'm stayin' in the game. 10. We all remember the hurricane of '94.

Page 111: Contraction Action
1. couldn't 2. won't 3. didn't 4. I'd 5. I'll 6. they'd 7. don't 8. they'll 9. wouldn't 10. they're 11. is not 12. it is 13. I have 14. she is 15. does not 16. shall not 17. has not 18. have not 19. you would 20. she will

Page 112: Say What?
1. The mayor said, "This will be the best and biggest race in the town's history." 2. One leading contender asked, "Will there be a large crowd?" 3. "There will be at least half of the town at the race," the mayor said. 4. Did anyone hear the organizers say, "We expect to see a thousand people there"? 5. "The race will start at Ocean Drive and end at Hill Crest Road," said the race's director. 6. "I am confident that I will win," said Garrett Billings from Oklahoma. 7. "Do you know how difficult it is to train for this?" asked racer Gail Bradley. 8. Will there be people around to help a racer if he or she says, "I need water"? 9. "I bring my entire family to see the race," says Ryan Vandorse. 10. "Whoever wins this race will have a good shot at the Olympics," said the race's director.

Page 113: Carry on the Conversation
Possible answers:
1. "You did, but I still made the runs," said Paul 2. "Did you hear the coach say, 'Paul couldn't have done that without Nate's help'?" 3. "Yes, you helped, but I can run faster than you can," said Paul. 4. Nate responded, "Maybe you can, but I can hit the ball farther than you can." 5. "No you can't," said Paul. 6. "Did you see me hit the ball in practice today?" said Nate. 7. "Well, okay, maybe you are good at hitting the ball," said Paul. 8. "Thank-you. Maybe you are faster than I am," said Nate 9. "Didn't you hear our parents say, 'Both Nick and Paul are great players'?" 10. Nate looked at Paul and said, "Yes, I did. We're both very good, and it's silly to fight about it."

Page 114: Popping Parentheses
2. We showed our approval **(clapping loudly)** of the musician's performance. 3. I live on a quiet side street **(Wildrose Street)** on the west side of town. 4. I left my coat **(the gray one)** at Joanne's house. 5. The girl called the sparrow **(using a bird call)** to her. 6. We made it home **(running quickly)** before the rain started. 7. I am going to my favorite city **(Montreal)** next week. 8. We saw our neighbor **(Mr. Neale)** working around his bushes. 9. I received good grades **(A's and B's)** on my report card. 10. We made a disturbance **(laughing loudly)** in the hallway.

Page 115: Capture the Colons
Draw circles around the colons in the following sentences:
1, 4, 6, 10

Page 116: Shopping List
Possible answers:
1. You should bring the following to the mountain: ski poles, skis, and sunglasses. 2. We saw a few animals this morning: rabbits, chipmunks, and squirrels. 3. They have my favorite flavors: chocolate, vanilla, and strawberry. 4. Dad keeps a few tools in that drawer: a hammer, nails, and a screwdriver. 5. Jacob's Market sells candy: jelly beans, licorice, and bubblegum. 6. The jeweler had some beautiful stones: rubies, emeralds, and diamonds. 7. A photographer never leaves home without this equipment: a camera, film, and a case. 8. I want to be one of the following when I am older: a doctor, a dentist, or a ballerina. 9. A painter needs the following: a brush, canvas, and paint. 10. We saw a few things next to the barn: a pitchfork, hay, and seeds.

Page 117: Slip in a Semicolon
1. My dentist likes crocodiles; there are pictures of crocodiles hanging on his ceiling. 2. A couple of snowflakes landed on my tongue; catching snowflakes is a lot of fun. 3. We arrived at the dance late; I want to be early next time. 4. My cousin bought a new skateboard; I wish I were old enough to have one. 5. The kangaroo jumped over the fence; kangaroos can jump very, very high. 6. I saw a seal in the harbor this morning; however, I only saw it for a second. 7. The water in the pitcher is too cold; my teeth are very sensitive. 8. We saw a flock of birds fly over us; they must be flying south for the winter. 9. I want to ride the yellow bumper cars; I wish that I had brought more money. 10. I gave Tania the yellow one; maybe I will get a blue one the next time.

Page 118: Semicolons Go Marching
1. We took a boat ride; roasted vegetables, hot dogs, and marshmallows; and lay in the sun. 2. The mechanic tested the brakes, the steering wheel, and the horn; fixed the engine; and replaced the headlight. 3. We could skate on the pond, in the arena, or on the lake; go sledding; or build a snow fort. 4. Michael and Megan packed sunscreen, bathing suits, and towels; drove to the beach; and swam with Tim, Sheri, and Kyle. 5. I like to play dominoes, checkers, and chess; read books; and watch television. 6. My cat likes to play with yarn, balls, and cat toys; scratch the sofa; and sleep on my feet. 7. We drove five hours to the campsite; unpacked our tents, sleeping bags, and clothing; and finally went to bed. 8. The coach blew the whistle; pointed at Kim, Kayla, and Karen; and

then took them out of the game. 9. My parents drove us to camp; waved good-bye to my brother, my sister, and me; and then they drove away. 10. The author read from her latest book; signed some autographs for Sharif, Jason, and Keri; and then went home to start writing another book.

Page 119: Hy-phen-ate
3. ware-house 5. fail-ure 6. im-peach 9. re-gion
10. ivo-ry 12. pil-grim 14. uto-pia 16. in-crease

Page 120: Word-Maker!
Possible answers:

ex-boss, brand-new car, faded-blue dress, half-sister, white-washed fence, all-purpose cleaner, spider-proof cellar, great-grandfather, big-grin look, self-made person

Page 121: Helpful Hyphens
1. My mom bought some fat-free ice cream for dessert. 2. I have only cleaned one-fourth of the windows. 3. Do you like your steak well-done? 4.The police officer wears a bullet-proof vest. 5. I have a t-ball game at noon tomorrow. 6. One-third of my well-worn jeans is covered in mud. 7. The cookies were half-baked, so they were a little soft. 8. My dog only ate one-fourth of its meal. 9. I have already sent you an e-mail about it. 10. We had a first-class cruise to Aruba. 12. su-per 13. iden-ti-ty 14. di-ver 16. ig-nore 17. en-vi-ron-ment 18. dan-ger

Page 122: A Sudden Dash!
1. We went to a park—I may have already told you this—to listen to a concert. 2. We brought along a picnic—we always do—so that we could stay there the whole day. 3. My three best friends came with me—you know them—along with my dog Ralph. 4. There was a large crowd—there always is—to see the band. 5. The band plays a mix of music—in case you didn't know—that appeals to many people. 6. We put our blanket near the pond—we like the water—and sat down. 7. We had a large blue blanket—you know which one—that everyone could sit on. 8. There were birds in the pond nearby—as there always are—that made some noise. 9. The concert started late—I was a little annoyed—but everyone was happy to hear the music. 10. Suddenly, my cat Ralph took off—you know how that cat likes to run—into the field to chase the mice!

Page 123: We Interrupt This Program . . .
1. I broke three parts of my body—my arm, my leg, and my ankle—when I fell off the roof. 2. We only go to my grandmother's house for one holiday—Christmas—during the school year. 3. I have many hobbies—building toys, racing cars, and playing baseball—that I enjoy. 4. You can buy many things—paper towels, vegetables, and hammers—at the general store. 5. I want to visit many cities—Paris, London, Hong Kong—during my lifetime.

Place a dash after the following sentences:
6, 9, 11, 12, 14

Page 124: A Barrel of Brackets
1. A doctor is quoted as saying that "one hospital has too many beds, while the other [Waldorf County Hospital] has too few." 2. Mrs. Stimpson, a local elementary school teacher, said "My school [Lyndon Elementary] needs renovations." 3. Mr. Blackwell, the fire chief, is quoted as saying "Mr. Shirwell, the new fireman [at Firehouse 80] will be a good fit." 4. Mr. Cox, the principal, told an assembly of teachers this morning that "Mrs. Bonny, [the retiring teacher at Sherwood Elementary] will be sorely missed." 5. The governor told the Clarksville City Council on Tuesday that he wouldn't "drop funding for either Morrisville or [his town] Clarksville." 7. The clown said that he "always [tries] to make people laugh if [he] can." 8. The artist said that she "[paints] landscapes more often than people." 9. The construction worker explained that the work "will continue until [his] men are finished." 10. We have a long drive, so the bus driver said that we could eat "as long as [he doesn't] have to clean anything up."

Page 125: Finishing Touches
1. Did you hear the news about the world's largest slide? 2. My little sister was born on May 10, 1997, in Tulsa, Oklahoma. 3. Be careful of the long, jagged stick in the road. 4. Wow, this is going to be fantastic! 5. Yes, I think that completing a marathon is a wonderful goal. 6. Jane, would you bring these plates to Uncle Harry? 7. We moved to Portland, Oregon, in late December. 8. If you want to see the space shuttle lift-off, you should go to Florida. 9. Ouch, that crab's claws really hurt! 10. We ate dinner, washed the dishes, and went to bed. 11. Rebecca, the sticky, slimy, gooey mess must be cleaned up now. 12. My Aunt Robin, a wonderful artist, painted all of our portraits. 13. When you are at camp, would you write to me? 14. Oh no, that is terrible, shocking news! 15. I picked some berries, and then I made a mud pie.

Page 126: Missing Marks
1. I ate all of Cheryl's ice cream when she wasn't looking. 2. Dad said, "Don't leave without saying good-bye." 3. Did you hear Tim say, "This house is haunted"? 4. The boys' team practices in the afternoon. 5. The children's toys are in the playroom downstairs. 6. I can't borrow Casey's skateboard because it's broken. 7. "Don't use all of the pepper," Dad said. 8. Gus's house is down the street from a cemetery. 9. We should bring the Smith's dog inside the house. 10. The rabbit's fur is a beautiful shade of gray. 11. I took Mark and David's place in line. 12. "Why can't you bring Ralph's surfboard to the beach?" said Nancy. 13. "You shouldn't sleep in the tent tonight," said

Jackie. 14. The band's instruments are still on the bus. 15. We couldn't bring all of the girls' shoes.

Page 127: Punctuation Panic!

1. I want a few things from the store: lettuce, ketchup, and blueberries. 2. My aunt loves to go waterskiing; she should buy a boat. 3. I took the test on Friday; I hope I passed. 4. Please bring the following items: duct tape, a screwdriver, and a saw. 5. My mom always uses the same ingredients: butter, flour, and eggs. 6. The winner said that "[he] trained long and hard for the race." 7. One of the wheels on your bike—if you didn't notice—is flat. 8. We watched the waves break on a blue-green sea. 9. My dream—you may already know this—is to be a jet pilot. 10. The clown said that "[he] liked to make people laugh, so [he] joined the circus." 11. My great-aunt is staying at our house next week. 12. We ate one-fourth of the pie and saved the rest for later. 13. I have a t-shirt—you may have seen it—that says "Smile." 14. The singer was a little off-key this afternoon. 15. The little dog—you know which one I mean—ran away this morning.

SUBJECTS AND PREDICATES

Page 128: Spotlight the Subjects

1. Carrie 2. Brad 3. they 4. Mrs. Ratchet 5. Mark 6. Wendy 7. She 8. He 9. Marty 10. Rabbits 11. ball 12. We 13. watch 14. Sergio 15. apples

Page 129: Something to Talk About

Subjects are bold:

Our Museum Trip

Yesterday, **we** went to the city. **We** went to see an exhibit at the museum. The **exhibit** was on the Mayan ruins. Our **family** read about it in the paper. **We** thought that it looked interesting.

We had to drive for a long time to get to the city. My **brother** got carsick twice. My **sister** played games. My **mother** helped me find license plates from different states. **Everyone** just wanted to get to the city.

The **search** for a parking space in the city took a long time. **Mom** found a sign for a parking garage, and **we** left it there. **I** was in charge of remembering the location.

The **museum** was very far from the parking garage. **We** had to walk a long way. My **feet** hurt from walking. After an hour, my **family** finally reached the museum. The **steps** up to the museum were steep and tiring. **We** were all exhausted.

Something looked odd in the museum. The **police** were inside looking around. **We** didn't see too many tourists. My **father** asked what happened. Oh no! Several **artifacts** on exhibit had been stolen! **We** never got to see the exhibit. The **authorities** are still looking for the culprit

and the artifacts.

Page 130: Savvy Subjects

1. Perhaps our teacher <u>Mrs. Jenkins</u> will sing for us at the concert. 2. Yesterday my best <u>friend</u> came into our store. 3. <u>I</u> would love to ride on your new bicycle! 4. The newest <u>house</u> on the block is falling apart! 5. Maybe the ballpoint <u>pens</u> would work better. 6. The sticky <u>mess</u> smells awful! 7. <u>We</u> heard some very beautiful music. 8. Susan's mother's <u>friend</u> is coming, too. 9. Our old <u>grill</u> is practically falling over. 10. A brand new <u>convertible</u> just drove by. 11. The baby <u>fish</u> are tickling my toes. 12. My best friend, <u>Jack</u>, gave Kara a flower. 13. My dad's <u>computer</u> is broken. 14. My mom's <u>cousins</u> always bring seafood to the family reunion. 15. The little gray <u>mouse</u> scampered across the floor.

Page 131: A Peppering of Predicates
A Delicious Dinner

I <u>watch</u> the cooks at the restaurant. Dana <u>chops</u> the vegetables into small pieces. Then he <u>puts</u> them into the frying pan. He <u>turns</u> the heat to high. He <u>cooks</u> the vegetables. The vegetables <u>look</u> scrumptious!

Rick <u>peels</u> potatoes with his potato peeler. He <u>cuts</u> them into chunks. He <u>sprinkles</u> salt and pepper on them. Then he <u>roasts</u> them in a pan in the oven. He <u>places</u> them on the top rack by the burner. The potatoes <u>turn</u> brown and crisp. They <u>taste</u> delicious!

Alice <u>prepares</u> the fish. She <u>removes</u> all of the scales from the fish. She <u>chops</u> off the head with her knife. Then she <u>slices</u> the fish down the middle. She <u>takes</u> out all of the bones. Then she <u>cooks</u> it in a pan. She <u>flips</u> the fish occasionally. She <u>watches</u> it carefully. She <u>squeezes</u> a little lemon juice on the fish. The fish <u>smells</u> yummy! The diners <u>enjoy</u> their dinner. They <u>agree</u>. The dinner <u>tastes</u> delicious.

Page 132: Precious Predicates

1. dug 2. rides 3. melted 4. painted 5. skipped 6. whistle 7. whispered 8. climbed 9. crossed 10. wished 11. turned 12. slipped 13. squeak 14. smell 15. bakes

Page 133: Choose a Predicate

Possible answers:

1. watches 2. contribute 3. revealed 4. shrieked 5. asked 6. shielded 7. traded 8. demanded 9. broke 10. pounced

Page 134: Subjects Versus Predicates

Subject, predicate:

1. girls, laugh 2. animal, falls 3. We, rode 4. monkeys, make 5. uncle, coughs

Possible answers:

6. The Queen of England offered to buy me lunch. 7. The caterpillar crawled up my sleeve onto my neck. 8. Mr. Snider consumed three large sandwiches. 9. The crafty

detective investigated the string of burglaries. 10. The giant's foot crushed the roof of our garage.

Page 135: Subject and Predicate Hunt

Subject, predicate:

1. whale, blew 2. bracelet, pinched 3. glasses, are
4. we, rolled 5. camera, broke 6. students, participated
7. decorator, converted 8. boat, drifted 9. wool, irritated
10. plant, sprouted 11. players, made 12. family, hummed
13. engineer, surveyed 14. defendant, jumped 15. players, dive

Page 136: Is It Natural?

1. N 2. I 3. I 4. N 5. N 6. I 7. I 8. I 9. N 10. I

Page 137: The Natural Way

1. My mom cried, "I need some iced tea!" 2. Sandra has heard the latest news about the mayor. 3. Five jellybeans were on the table. 4. The word *can* is even more important. 5. Mrs. Jacobs whispered, "I am going insane!" 6. The lonely horseman rode over the hill and through the woods. 7. The grave of my great-great-grandfather lies there. 8. The bat flew into the window. 9. The stain on your dress is even more noticeable. 10. The statue of the greatest woman alive stands here.

Page 138: What's the Difference?

1. N 2. N 3. I 4. N 5. I 6. I 7. I 8. N 9. N 10. I

Possible answers:

11. The storm blew all of our windows shut. 12. Has Mrs. Smith cooked the roast? 13. My brothers raced to the front of the line. 14. The players all hit the ball very hard. 15. There are many seagulls on the beach.

Page 139: Be Agreeable!

1. paint 2. shrinks 3. plays 4. eat 5. race 6. insist
7. smells 8. solve 9. competes 10. suggest

Page 140: Let's Go to the Movies!

1. Are 2. wants 3. dislike 4. sees 5. is 6. cry 7. shines
8. go 9. watches 10. does

Page 141: Check It Out!

The following sentences agree:

1, 3, 6, 8, 11, 13, 14, 15

Page 142: The Show Must Go On!

Subject, predicate:

1. Kiley, makes 2. play, is 3. actors, have 4. director, wants 5. lights, shine 6. parents, volunteer 7. actors, come 8. crowds, come 9. director, says 10. Everyone, hopes 11. camera, films 12. seats, are 13. band, plays 14. audience, surrounds 15. people, work

Page 143: Pop Quiz!

1. S: seal, P: dove 2. S: coins, P: sink 3. S: acorns, P: fell

4. S: we, P: saw 5. S: Cynthia, P: likes 6. N 7. I 8. I
9. N, welcome 10. I, sits 11. N, refer 12. I 13. N 14. I
15. I, does

SENTENCES, CLAUSES, PHRASES, AND PARAGRAPHS

Page 144: Park Plans

The following sentences are declarative:

1, 2, 3, 5, 6, 8, 9, 10, 11, 13, 14

Page 145: Curious Clara

Possible answers:

1. Why are you going? 2. What is the most popular place in Chicago? 3. What did the whale look like? 4. Do whales usually swim alone or in groups? 5. How much snow will we get? 6. How is snow formed? 7. How do bees make honey? 8. How do you collect the honey? 9. What did he talk about? 10. Did the astronaut go to the moon?

Page 146: Beach Rules

The following sentences are imperative:

1, 2, 4, 5, 7, 8, 11, 13, 14, 15

Page 147: Fun in the Sea!

The following sentences are exclamatory:

1, 2, 4, 5, 6, 8, 10, 11, 12, 14

Page 148: Sentence Sleuth

1. question mark, I 2. period, D 3. question mark, I
4. period, M 5. exclamation point, E 6. period, D
7. exclamation point, E 8. period, M 9. exclamation point, E 10. period, D 11. question mark, I 12. period, M
13. exclamation point, E 14. period, D 15. question mark, I

Page 149: I.D. the Sentences

1. T, question mark 2. T, period 3. F, exclamation point
4. T, period 5. F, question mark 6. F, exclamation point
7. F, period 8. T, period 9. T, period 10. F, exclamation point 11. F, question mark 12. F, period 13. F, period
14. F, exclamation point 15. T, period

Page 150: Is It Simple?

1. S 2. S 3. C 4. S 5. S 6. C 7. C 8. S 9. S 10. C

Page 151: Sentence Construction

Possible answers:

1. Bob likes to go waterskiing, but he can't go very often.
2. They don't have any more shampoo; I can't wash my hair without it. 3. I am leaving for camp tomorrow, and my sister is coming with me. 4. We could fish at the lake, or we could fish in the river. 5. I want to paint a picture, but I don't have any more paint. 6. The dog chewed on

my homework, and it ate our dessert. 7. My uncle bought a plane; I wish I were old enough to fly it. 8. We could play in the backyard, or we could play at the neighbor's house. 9. The flowers in their yard are turning brown, and they're falling over. 10. My mom is taking me to the baseball game, and she is going to buy me a hot dog.

Page 152: Tie Them Together
1. Valerie bought eight raffle tickets, but I won the prize.
2. My rabbit hopped out of the cage, and it ate all of our carrots. 3. Jason and Tim bought new bikes; I wish I could ride them. 4. We could eat candy, or we could make dinner. 5. I want those baseball cards, but I don't have enough money.

Page 153: Make It Complex
2. The gold and silver box, which we found on the street, contains a lot of money. 3. You may choose a sugar cereal, whichever you want, for your birthday. 4. Because we ran out of gas, our car stopped running. 5. After you finish your homework, you may go to the park. 6. When he is finished making dinner, he will make dessert. 7. My sister, whose shirt I am wearing, has very good fashion sense. 8. I bought some ice cream, after you told me to buy it, at the grocery store. 9. While the band was practicing, I couldn't hear you talk. 10. The man in the corner, who was dancing, is the cousin of my best friend's father.

Page 154: From Simple to Complex
1. Because it's warm outside, we can't go skiing. 2. That girl, who is sitting at the corner table, is my brother's girlfriend. 3. You may buy one game, whichever you want, at the store. 4. After I finish my chores, I can go outside to play. 5. While you were sleeping, you snored very loudly. 6. My father, whose camera I'm using, is a great photographer. 7. Before I had the pie, I ate a turkey sandwich. 8. Buy some soda, whatever you'd like, at the grocery store. 9. We bought ice cream, which we ate rapidly, at the fair. 10. Since Karen can't come here, we should go to Karen's house.

Page 155: Complex Charades
1. f 2. d 3. g 4. a 5. h 6. e 7. j 8. i 9. c 10. b

Page 156: Sentence Type?
1. SS 2. SS 3. CX 4. CP 5. CP 6. SS 7. CX 8. SS 9. CX 10. CP

Page 157: So Many Sentences
1. SS 2. CP 3. CP 4. SS 5. CX 6. CP 7. CX 8. CP 9. SS 10. CX

Page 158: Abracadabra!
Possible answers:

1. The rabbits, which are very feisty, escaped out of their cage. 2. I want to go on the ride. 3. We could bring along

some apples, or we could bring some peaches. 4. My sister got a new scooter. 5. After making a wish, I blew out the candles on the cake. 6. I love to go fishing, but no one wants to come with me. 7. I saw the baby, who looks like Tania, at the park with her mom. 8. I am moving to New York City. 9. Because I was happy, I wrote two songs this morning. 10. Kim has a camp on Cliff Island; we go there often.

Page 159: They Can Stand Alone!
The following are independent clauses:
1, 3, 4, 5, 6, 9, 11, 12

Page 160: Be Independent!
Possible answers:

1. Green, slimy snakes slither around my yard. 2. Super-squishy sponges are in the cupboard. 3. My best friend Rick likes baseball. 4. Summer vacation last year was a blast. 5. Wake up your brother. 6. The deep-sea diver saw a shipwreck. 7. Bring a hammer to your father. 8. Hamburgers and hot dogs taste yummy. 9. Look for a pearl earring. 10. My sunglasses are in the car.

Page 161: I Depend on You
The following are dependent clauses:
1, 3, 5, 6, 9, 10, 11, 12

Page 162: Do You Depend on Me?
The following are dependent clauses:
1, 3, 4, 5, 8, 9, 10, 11

Possible answers:

1. Before you order, check the menu. 3. Since we can't see, turn up the light. 4. We were out while the water was running. 5. We will be there, unless we can't go. 8. The alarm was loud, although I didn't hear it. 9. Do not touch the wire because it is hot. 10. After you finish that, start on the next group. 11. Be sure to seal the hole so that it doesn't leak.

Page 163: Independent or Dependent?
1. D 2. I 3. D 4. D 5. I 6. I 7. D 8. I 9. D 10. I

Page 164: More and More Clauses
The following are independent clauses:
2, 5, 6, 8, 9, 11

Page 165: A Picnic of Prepositions
Prepositions are italicized:

1. *underneath* Cheryl's bed 2. *upon* the flat rocks
3. *Throughout* the evening 4. *toward* the left side
5. *inside* the cabin 6. *below* the deck 7. *between* my aunt and uncle 8. *near* the sidelines 9. *onto* the counter
10. *through* the tunnels 11. *at* the museum 12. *from* Sweden 13. *during* the concert 14. *aboard* the USS *Cole*

15. *within* the limits

Page 166: Play Ball!

The following prepositional phrases should be circled:

1. of friends, on the playground 2. to Cindy 3. toward the swings 4. past the recess teacher 5. under the swing 6. between Trevor and Nancy 7. with his glove 8. across the playground 9. near the fence 10. to Mike, to Cindy

Page 167: The Treasure Chest

Preposition, object:

1. above, garage 2. beneath, blanket 3. inside, lock 4. toward, ceiling 5. out, top 6. between, books 7. around, books 8. toward, back 9. toward, front 10. among, shoes 11. from, chest 12. with, knife 13. Inside, envelope 14. from, grandmother; to, father 15. until, end

Page 168: Pop-Up Phrases

Objects are italicized:

1. on the museum *steps* 2. under the *scaffolding* 3. through the *gates* 4. below the *decks* 5. Without a *doubt* 6. off the *grass* 7. between the *signs* 8. down the *hall* 9. against the *tide* 10. until the last *moment*

Page 169: Shade the Parts

Prepositions; objects; words that modify

1. underneath; bridges; three 2. toward; front; the 3. on; ground; the *and* outside; store; the, grocery 4. between; chairs; the, two 5. on; pond; the 6. around; flowerbed; your 7. down; hill; the, small 8. past; site; the, construction 9. during; storm; the 10. at; fair; the

Page 170: Fragment Repair

Possible answers:

2. That is not my favorite salad. 3. Sandra is bringing ketchup and mayonnaise. 4. Your soup is very good. 5. I like to cook once in a while. 6. That animal eats nuts and berries. 7. My mom washes the vegetables before we eat them. 8. Those look like very comfortable shoes. 9. Chocolate cheesecake is always a good choice. 10. Josh always tries to climb the tree, but he isn't tall enough.

Page 171: What's Missing?

2. subject 3. subject and verb 4. subject 5. subject and verb 6. subject and verb 7. subject 8. subject and verb 9. subject

Possible answers:

10. Cynthia never goes camping. 11. Rocco chases the dog. 12. The food is not very good. 13. Evelyn yells loudly. 14. The lights in the kitchen are never bright. 15. This is a hot and sticky afternoon. 16. My step-father reels in big fish. 17. This painting is not my best work.

18. My uncle sleeps during the day and works at night.

Page 172: Catch the Run-Ons!

Possible answers:

1. The friends played some music, and they sang some songs. 2. The dog chewed my sneakers, but it didn't touch the pie. 3. The grass is growing quickly, so it needs to be mowed more often. 4. My watch fell in the pool, but I don't think it is broken. 5. I will buy some lettuce; I will make a salad. 6. We should buy some salsa, and we should make some quesadillas. 7. We could play darts, or we could play checkers. 8. The lawn mower is loud; it is annoying. 9. I could call you, or you could call me. 10. I saw a fire engine, but it was far away.

Page 173: Run Down the Run-Ons
Finding Lacey

Jason and Patrick watered Mr. McIntyre's plants every time he went away. Mr. McIntyre had a lot of plants in his house, and he also had a garden in the backyard. He had roses, daisies, lilies, and peonies in his flower garden; he had tomatoes and cucumbers in his vegetable garden. It usually took Jason and Patrick an hour to finish all of the watering.

Mr. McIntyre had a dog; her name was Lacey. Lacey was a big golden retriever who loved to chase birds but never caught any. Jason and Patrick loved Lacey, but they knew they couldn't take her outside to play. Mr. McIntyre had strictly forbidden it. They could ask Mrs. Walker to walk Lacey, or they could ask Mr. Spencer to do it. If Lacey got free of her leash, she was too fast and too strong for Jason and Patrick to catch her.

Jason and Patrick had been at Mr. McIntyre's house for an hour one day when they noticed that the porch door was wide open. They called for Lacey, but she didn't come. They hunted everywhere in the house for her. They looked in the basement, and they even looked in the attic. Jason said, "If she isn't in the house, then she has to be outside."

They looked everywhere outside for Lacey. They looked in the woods, and they looked up and down the street. They had almost given up hope when they heard her bark. They ran toward the bark, and they found Lacey in the flowerbed. She was stalking a bird that was sitting in the birdbath in the garden. They quietly walked toward her, and then they jumped to grab Lacey's collar. Lacey darted through the flowerbed and into the vegetable garden. Lacey tore up all of the flowers and vegetables, but they finally got a hold of her. What a mess!

Page 174: Let Them Run!

Answers will vary.

Page 175: Step 1: Topic Sentence

Possible answer:

Newspapers are a very good source of information.

Page 176: Step 2: Paragraph

Possible answer:

Too much junk food is not good for you. Junk food is often high in sugar and fat. Sugar decays your teeth, and too much fat can make you gain weight. Junk food doesn't have the nutrients that people need for healthy bodies. Instead of junk food, people should eat more fruits, vegetables, and grains. These foods will give you more energy and will last longer in your stomach. Too much junk food will fill you up, so you won't have any space left for the important foods. Just say *no* to junk food!

Page 177: Which Type Is It?

1. exclamatory, exclamation point 2. declarative, period
3. imperative, period 4. exclamatory, exclamation point
5. interrogative, question mark 6. declarative, period
7. interrogative, question mark 8. exclamatory,
exclamation point 9. declarative, period 10. exclamatory,
exclamation point 11. compound 12. simple 13. complex
14. compound 15. complex

Page 178: Name It, Create It!

Answers and possible sentences:

1. declarative, compound; There are sixty minutes in an hour, and there are sixty seconds in a minute.
2. imperative, simple; Take me to the store.
3. exclamatory, simple; Wow, these shoes are so cool!
4. declarative, complex; If it were snowing, I would go sledding. 5. exclamatory, simple; Watch out for the ice!
6. interrogative, complex; When I return, do you want to go to Connecticut? 7. imperative, simple; Pass me the mustard. 8. interrogative, compound; Do you want to bring it, or should I bring it? 9. declarative, simple; There are too many plates in the cupboard. 10. exclamatory, simple; Look out for Bigfoot!

Page 179: Find the Missing Pieces

1. If I lived near the beach, I would learn to surf. 2. I will watch the children, and I will eat my lunch. 3. I already put the peanut butter in the cabinet. 4. When I go to Mark's house, I want to listen to music. 5. I emptied the wastebasket into the large garbage bag. 6. I will help you with your homework, but you must do the work. 7. The kittens looked identical, so I didn't know which was yours.
8. Jeffrey eats pasta with a spoon. 9. The baseball rolled past the pitcher to the third baseman. 10. *The Home of the Lions* was not a good movie.

Page 180: Search for Clues

Problems; possible corrections:

1. dependent clause; When you see Mr. Radshaw, tell him I said hello. 2. fragment; Terry thinks he can lift the big armchair. 3. prepositional phrase; I signed the letter and put it inside the envelope. 4. prepositional phrase; I will go skiing down the mountain if you come along. 5. run-on; I want to travel to England, and I want to meet the queen. 6. fragment; I had a very good time. 7. dependent clause; If you want ketchup, you should bring it.
8. fragment; The tuba is not a small instrument. 9. run-on; You should read the book, or you should watch the movie. 10. run-on; Because there aren't any more seats, I'll sit on the floor. 11. prepositional phrase; A bat just flew over my head! 12. fragment; The little boy waits by the side of the road for the bus. 13. dependent clause; When you go upstairs, would you bring my sweater with you? 14. run-on; The boy over there, who brought us our water, is a very good waiter. 15. prepositional phrase; Fifteen clowns climbed into the car!